The
Sales Hiring
Handbook

For technology originators, manufacturers, sales organizations and others who want improved sales productivity from their organization.

A guide for hiring VP of Sales, Directors of Sales and Marketing, Account Executives, and Business Development representatives for your business.

This reference book highlights how to avoid costly mistakes in hiring sales people for your organization. It also answers the question, "When does it make sense to bring in professionals who specialize?"

This book includes phone interviewing techniques, first and second interview questions, and even some self-analysis for reviewing your sales processes. Is your company sales driven? A highly traveled, executive-level headhunter shares numerous hiring stories to learn from.

The McCandlish Group
www.mccandlishgroup.com
614-766-1800

Printed by Signature Book Printing, www.sbpbooks.com

Acknowledgements

My family is my support group and life's blood. I have to be the luckiest Dad in the world and welcome the chance to catch up to my kids' achievements.

I take every chance to brag about them and whether you're interested or not, here they are.

Joe; an attorney with a regional services company, Andy; completed his PHD at Princeton in molecular genetics, Lynda; Lacrosse scholarship athlete at Northwestern University with 2 national championships and International traveler, Kristin; Economics grad from Northwestern with 4 National Ladies lacrosse titles, and Caz; our future television superstar.

My wife Eileen has been with me through thick and thin. An Internationally known interior designer and successful business operator, her continued support has given new meaning to the phrase "life partner."

Many thanks to Robin Fritts, workout partner, friend and most positive person on the planet. Also a special thanks to my sister and friend, Lavi Clausen, selling real estate in Lake Geneva, Wisconsin. She has an amazing talent of making immediate friends with everyone in the room.

Great thanks and gratitude to the many entrepreneurial companies from which I've learned life's lessons and also thanks to all past mentors and managers for your time spent with me and the dreams and experiences we shared.

Table of Contents

Author's bio

Mike's sales career began in 1980 as a home security sales representative. After learning to cold call in residential neighborhoods, he became proficient at one-call closing and soon was promoted into management.

The next move was selling Canon copiers. He developed a geographic territory and was promoted into a key accounts position.

In May of 1985, when Cellular One activated their system in Columbus, Ohio, Mike was named Director of Sales and Marketing. He established the first dealer network, coordinated public relations and implemented sales training programs for the exciting start-up technology.

The entrepreneurial bug bit him as he developed PHONES TO GO, a cellular business in 1986. As Ohio's top sales agent, they were purchased by Cellular One in 1989.

In the fall of 1989 Mike established MCCANDLISH MARKETING as a video distribution company with representation agreement for Quest Entertainment of Universal Studios in Orlando. The company serviced Kroger, West Coast Video, and Blockbuster. As Quest's top distributor, he conducted training seminars for new Quest distributors; representing specialty lines including "how to" videos and non-theatrical release feature films. The company was sold in 1995.

Mike then joined International Profit Associates and sold management-consulting services to small and medium-sized businesses. He was the company's #1 cash collector of 400 outside sales consultants in 1997 and set a domestic record of 18 sales in one week. He was promoted to Regional Director of Mergers and Acquisitions and managed 30 consultants in the Midwest Territory. IPA grew from 19 employees in 1991 to 2000 in 2002 with annual sales of $180,000,000 and earned Inc. 500 "Fastest Growing" status.

In 1999 THE MCCANDLISH GROUP was founded. The executive search firm specializes in business development positions, including Sales and Marketing from the account executive level to Director and VP. They've successfully handled searches at IBM, Cisco, Bank One, Sterling Commerce, Qwest and numerous small technology-based organizations.

In all, Mike has trained over 1000 sales representatives to sell products or services in 7 different industries; Construction, Cellular, Home Security, Office Equipment, Management Consulting, the Entertainment Industry and Staffing.

Introduction

This handbook is written for anyone who hires job candidates for sales related positions. The book's purpose is to guide you in making the best hiring decisions, thus protecting your bottom line. Hiring the wrong salesperson, manager or executive can cost your company in many areas; time spent, dissention among ranks, miscommunication with existing or potential clients, and misquoting your services to actually cost you money.

Let's face facts!!! Do you realize how important the field communicator of your product or service is? You've heard it before, NOTHING HAPPENS unless they make the sale! You can't pay the rent, feed the employees, and maintain whoever answers the phone. And if salespeople don't sell, you'll have to decide who doesn't continue employment with your company or division next month.

If you're a manager or owner, you may not like, trust or understand sales people but one thing is fact...*your attitude towards sales people and your management of them will dictate the growth and operation of your enterprise.*

Hiring the right sales candidate is the first step to ensure your success.

How do you know the person sitting across the desk will work as hard as they now promise? How can you derive the right answers from their references? Should you give sales candidates a test? Which test? Just because they made quota at The Wonderful Stuff Software Company will they make their number with your product? Are you asking the right questions?

"Hey Mike," you say. "You're the headhunter, I'll pay you to steal a sales person from my competitor. I don't want to call over there but I don't mind if you do."

Let me ask, if I'm going to bring over a competitor's sales person, are you prepared to pay them higher commissions? Give them more flextime? Pay a greater portion of their benefits? Give them a nicer car and pay for gas and lunches? Pay their country club tabs? Where does it end? Then you have to deal with insiders like production people who say, "Shouldn't I get a raise if you're going to give this guy something off the charts and he's never even worked for us? I've been here 7 years"...and so on and so forth.

Also, how are you going to create outside the box thinking if you keep hiring your competitor's salespeople? After you pay their legal fees for violating their non-compete you're already starting at a deficit.

Besides, there's no guarantee they match your culture and can sell in your environment.

What's the answer? It's three-fold.

First, there are occasionally salespeople from competitors who may work out because you're a better cultural match and they can earn more because of the environment you've created for sales people to thrive. You and the candidate, with help from key staff, can analyze that during the interview process, but remember it's your decision. Too often the sales candidate is "selling" you because of their financial needs. Remember though, being appreciated goes farther than all the questions and issues I mentioned above. If the sales candidate is selling hard, it could be because they see your environment is better for them. And you should ask them specifically what they visualize.

Second, recruiting and hiring sales performers from companies who hire at entry level and implement extensive training can be beneficial. Maintaining your own sales training program on your products or services can be expensive so this has some merit. If another company teaches sales process and technique, you can benefit. Normally you could pay higher commissions than the "sales trainers" because their training program is costing them.

You're still a few steps away because salespeople, even at the highest levels, still must be managed. The process itself must be managed. And if you are not capable to manage the sales stars of the world, don't attempt it. They will break your heart with good intentions you call unkept promises. Hiring a qualified sales manager has more appeal if you learn how to manage the manager.

A strong manager will keep you out of trouble and ensure sales activities. When you learn how to manage the sales manager and know the right questions to ask, you've increased your chances of growing your enterprise profitably.

Third, THE KEY is to hire people who are motivated to do the job. Not the ones that SHOULD, not the ones that CAN, but the ones that are MOTIVATED to do so.

Until you learn the questions to ask and what to listen for in their answers, you're always going to make sales hiring mistakes and waste company resources.

Do your interview questions consider the sales candidate's motivation for the job? They should, because it's the most important aspect of the process.

It's your thinking...

I've heard so many hiring managers say, "I didn't like him because he couldn't _____for me." This manager, in his infinite wisdom, is still looking for someone to do something for HIM. He doesn't get it. Salespeople won't do something for him or you, they sell for themselves! Your company's products and services are a chance for them to showcase their talents. You surely understand a salesperson's ticket to higher compensation is mostly from commissions, or should be. That makes them the only employees in the company that are on a similar pay plan as the owner. It's a risk and reward scenario.

Focus on being a good support function for them, treat them as customers, and you will thrive.

Now, many salespeople were drawn to a sales career because they liked people, were effective communicators, and they could work flexible hours and earn more money per hours worked.

From hiring sales people in 7 different industries and training over 1000 sales professionals and independents, I've decided to share tips and nuances of HOW TO.

Also, I occasionally use analogies of home building because so many people seem to identify with principles of home building and the differences between the production side and sales promises made. In reality The McCandlish Group works with technology originators in areas of software development, telecommunications, manufacturing and engineering. We enjoy assisting sales organizations in any industry.

After reading this handbook, you'll have the information you need to avoid pitfalls hiring managers make in sourcing the right sales talent for your enterprise. Best of luck!

ABOUT MOTIVATION

Since I believe motivation is the key to a successful employment match, I'd like to share this thought.

Every now and then you encounter someone who demonstrates excellence on the job. It might be an exceptional waitress who anticipates your every need. Or, it could be a manager who generates both high performance and loyalty from his teams. It could be a teacher with a knack for unlocking the desire to learn in each student.

Excellence, true excellence, is something we prize but seldom see. It's a joy to encounter someone who is truly excellent at what they do. Why is that so rare? More importantly, how can you become known as a man or woman who consistently demonstrates excellence?

One comment that is heard time and again about those who demonstrate excellence is, "He/she is a natural at it." They don't seem to struggle to be excellent; it just flows. That is always a sign of motivation, and therein lies the first key: Motivation is required for excellence.

Motivation is what we like to do naturally. It's like being right or left-handed. We don't have to think about it. The same is true for people known for excellence. They have a group of motivations that work in concert to help them perform at a higher level. Like all motivations, these were inborn and are as much a part of them as being blue-eyed or tall.

But there is a second key: Motivation can be developed. People who demonstrate excellence have identified their motivations and worked hard to develop them. They have added knowledge, skill, experience and practice to consistently produce at the highest levels.

By the way, there is a flip side to these two keys, and it is this: The best we can be with low motivation is adequate. No matter how hard we work and desire it, in the long run we will never be excellent at something without high levels of motivation in that area. In other words, if we toil in areas where we have low motivation, we resign ourselves to mediocrity.

Who wants to be mediocre? Who wants to be known as adequate? Wouldn't you rather have a shot at excellence? The first step to unlocking your excellence is to understand what you enjoy and know what you do well naturally. What are your motivations?

ARE YOU A SALES COMPANY?

Before we review questions to ask sales candidates and managers, please review some thoughts to evaluate yourself as a sales company. Top producing sales people are drawn to companies that have a sales mentality. That is, they are rewarded for sales performance, not punished.

Also, when recruiting top sales pros, there are certain companies that are known for sales "training grounds" that I look for. Companies like IBM, Xerox, HP, all have extensive training programs and drive their business through managing daily sales activities. Top VP of Sales candidates are cultured from those environments. When evaluating your sales hire, where they come from is a consideration.

Examples of sales rewards:

An *unannounced* "*gift*" *or* "*prize*" in front of peers for contributions above and beyond the call of duty will demonstrate appreciation. For example, an account executive spent extra time with a client for non-revenue producing but account retention activity.

Or

Send him/her and their spouse to dinner for a special effort or notable sale. Get the family involved and make the rep proud of the company he/she sweats for.

Have ongoing salesperson of the month contests. Small companies can name quarterly contributors if they have a long sales cycle, but put something out there continuously. Top companies motivate weekly, monthly or quarterly. Sales trips, trophies, cash, and clothing contests all motivate someone. It is sometimes difficult to monitor the exact effect, but most growth companies are using sales incentives.

Constantly recognize managers who re-sell their troops on the company products and services. A kind word of recognition goes a long way to show appreciation. Everyone knows you didn't have to recognize the effort..... but great sales organizations do, as part of their model.

Take this basic example. The CEO of a construction company who builds commercial facilities for health care organizations is the founder. He grew up with a hammer in his hand, measuring and re-measuring, and berating vendors who don't do it right the first time. He exudes good workmanship and is known for quality, seldom getting complaints. His customers are aware of his quality and they find him. Salespeople don't have to do much arm-twisting to make sales.

If salespeople mention the wrong material used, if they miscommunicate delivery dates, or promise extras that can't be delivered, the owner is irate. Sales people are not highly paid because the owner doesn't recognize sales effort, as his houses sell themselves.

The company growth has stalled because they've reached a level where they must prospect daily for new business. " Your company needs to be sales driven to grow. Examine your culture and let's put some new processes in place," I stressed to the owner.

He's convinced sales people are out to get him and bankrupt his company. "I'm not giving them higher commissions" he says, "they just take walk-in orders because our quality sells the home."

My response was "Then why are we talking?"

He finally admitted the problem; HIM. The product was "his baby". He has no idea how to manage sales people and faces daily reminders. "The sales department sold eight in one month and none in the next month. I can't schedule labor or purchasing to support them." He went on and on.

I said "Your culture is not sales- friendly. On the production side, project managers and construction supervisors are praised for quality builds with no complaints. Project managers receive bonuses for delivering final finished projects on time. That's fine. But, behind the scenes, you joke viciously about what salespeople say to customers. That gives approval for others to do the same."

"Your sales people are paid a low draw versus commission, generally unsupported by advertising and expected to generate most of their sales through referrals, cold calling and realtor relationships. It's a wonder you even have a sales force. They certainly don't look happy to be here. Don't you think potential home buyers see what I see?" I continued.

"OK, what do we need to do?" he mellowed.

"We need to hire a director of sales with a business-to-consumer background, probably residential construction, who understands marketing, sales management and customer service. We will implement a new training program for project managers and construction supervisors to adapt to the new sales approach," I started.

"WHAT?" the CEO seemed shocked.

"Sure," I continued. "The new sales manager will teach sales technique, and possibly home building 101 to the new sales people. They will learn how to prospect, practice presentations, develop commercial realtor relationship calls, write down and memorize presentations for smooth communication, and then you'll see more sales. Both product knowledge and selling skills are necessary for a successful operation."

I continued, "Product training should continue, but tailor the content towards what they have to know to make the sale. Their knowledge base should be more than the potential customer but not necessarily make sales people construction experts. We'd also have your construction supervisor do some training to develop a relationship basis and better resolve service issues. It'll be a better working atmosphere."

"The sales people will gain confidence from positive feedback from employees. They'll also be motivated from selling more, thus earning more. Make sense?"

I went on, "Also, we'll stress improvement of communication. When sales people quote inaccuracies, instead of humiliating them, the project manager will jot it down for later discussion in private and calmly handle the customer. Now, I'll ask you to let the sales manager manage and give you some questions to ask him every week. Do not have much interaction with the sales people other than 'good job and things will get better." And it did.

This basic scenario is a crude example or possible opportunity we may handle as an ancillary, free service. Sales issues are quickly obvious to us, as outsiders, when you may not see problems with procedures from the inside.

here we go...
I'll create anxiety when I say this but top sales organizations place emphasis on attracting, supporting, coddling, and keeping top salespeople at almost any cost. Those companies know and practice phrases such as "sales driven", and "sell it first, then figure out how to deliver."

Business owners often say, "What do I tell my other employees who do a great job. I won't make heroes of sales people when others are also doing a good job."

I might explain it to those business owners and technology originators like this.

If you do not sell more each year/month, growth will be impossible. Additionally, if no one buys your products, there will be no other positions in your business necessary. Now, your other employees are obviously important to the company but sales people play a different role than those with salaried positions. They take risks for a major part of their income (or if not, they should). It is not guaranteed.

Because of the need for new sales, great companies create an environment of virtually unlimited opportunity for sales people. Companies that do not recognize this are never market leaders and opportunities within their organizations are normally limited.

The McCandlish Group recognizes the importance of business development. I personally make time daily for daily out-bound prospecting calls. In our business, new clients are critical and if we don't do more searches each year we will stagnate and die.

How often do you introduce sales incentives?

I sold management-consulting services for a company that went from 19 employees in 1990 to 2000 in 2003. Their sales are now over 180 Million and EVERY DAY they have a sales incentive. Yes, every day. It is faxed to 400 virtual reps who are motivated daily to knock down doors, make presentations to business owners and have energy to be convincing and stress urgency.

This methodology was utilized to sell more today than yesterday, more this week than last, and more this month...you get the picture. You can boot your long-term plan if you continuously sell more each month and year. It's very much about the "short term".

They often added a spiff of $300.00 for a day with two first-call closes or a $500.00 drawing and drew names from a hat for everyone who made a sale that day.

With their process, I was able to sell 18 consulting engagements in one week. The outbound telemarketing operation set up three leads daily for outside reps that made presentations to business owners. The reps also set their own appointments but most relied on those furnished by the company.

Now, most sales cycles are longer than one-call close opportunities. So, in your enterprise identify what key activities convert to a sale? Is it a 30-day trial of your software? You can base an incentive on number of trials in a month or quarter. How about a weekend in Las Vegas for the most trials in a quarter? If the quarterly goal is 4 trials, then establish a team incentive of everyone who sells over 4 qualifies.

How about a software sale without a trial? Trials are costly since support is an issue. If an account executive gets a $200,000 order from referral selling or taking a potential client to an existing client installation, doesn't it save the enterprise thousands? It shows commitment to share the savings with the creative sales person.

The few companies that share command loyalty.

Example of sales punishment:

Re-assign a large account from a territorial rep and give it to the major account representative or inside sales.

Companies do this consistently to pay lower commissions and say it's a more effective way to handle the account. "Give them more specialized attention," they say. Possibly, but sales pros think it's unnecessary. If the sales rep has the initiative to open the account because they are motivated to do more or have appropriate contacts, then they can normally handle the account maintenance. If the policy is continued, the average account executive in your company will eventually be de-motivated and move on. *The customer bought from the representative partly because they wanted them to handle their account.*

You have taken away the atmosphere of unlimited opportunity and it's a kiss of death for the sales rep wanting a sky's the limit approach.

or

Cut the AE's territory for better penetration.

Be careful here. When you take something away, give something in return. If you take, even a small theft, it is perceived as huge or insurmountable to many sales types. They may have an attitude of understanding if the idea is properly sold to them. But, if you have to cut the territory, introduce a new product or service for them to profit on at the same time. Then it becomes a more viable strategy.

THE PHONE INTERVIEW

How do you set your interviews? Does your secretary, receptionist or office manager schedule them for you? Big mistake. You've taken away an opportunity to hear them ask for the appointment on an introductory call, something you'll be asking them to do.

Schedule your own appointments. The call should take on new meaning when you smile to yourself as you are grading them on their approach. Get to know each other a bit without the visual. It's effective.

Please talk with them on the phone whether they are in the same city or not. Remember the phone is for setting appointments and all salespeople need phone skills. It's essential.

A good question to ask immediately, is
1.Q: *What motivates you?* If the candidate is motivated by something other than what you offer, you can save some time, wish them good luck and say goodbye. Also, hesitation is not good here because sales people should know what motivates them.

2.Q: *Why do you want to work for our company?*
Listen for confusion or confidence. If they quickly start into why (and it sounds reasonable) or even answer honestly which may be "I don't know yet, but if we keep talking I can tell you if I do very soon." That's OK. Just determine if what you offer will motivate them or not.

3.Q: *Are you currently employed?*
As they tell you about their last position, or current job, keep things open-ended so they can expand the communication. IF

they start rambling, interrupt and get control again with another question or gain clarification on previous statements.

4. Q: If something makes your company different in the marketplace, get it out in the open early and see how they respond. Mention your sales process, briefly then...Q: *Can you visualize contributing in our business model? And then WHY this model, and HOW?*

5 Q: *Tell me your best personal sales story...* This should be instantaneous and interesting. They should be smiling as if remembering an old friend.

By the way, some phone screens last an hour or more, some are 10 minutes. The objective is a general skill set inquiry to determine mutual interest.

Everyone on a sales team will not be on the same page. Many are more selfish than others, and sometimes team players aren't selfish enough. It is not detrimental to have competing personalities on a team. You'll learn more about what really fits for your team by bringing in different personality types. Sometimes it hurts, but reps won't always love each other or even work for the common goal of putting the company first.

When I sold office copiers for a local independent Canon dealer, there were 19 salespeople in the office. It was fairly competitive. I found myself working harder when someone I didn't like made a big sale or received attention. It got my juices flowing similar to an athletic event.

One day, towards the end of the month. I walked in with two signed orders and was reviewing the month's productivity. Another rep was watching and said, "I heard you sold 7 this month. That's pretty good, but I sold 9."

I couldn't imagine this rep beating me on his best day so I

asked the sales manager. He said, "Well, I'm not sure what that rep sold but that sounds high."

I said, "Then why don't we have the sales numbers posted. Then the truth would prevail. It should also motivate others when they can see where they are."

The sales manager said, "We don't want to make the guys not selling look bad. Keeping reps is difficult."

I said, "You're kidding. This is very competitive in the field and we have to cold call all day to get business. I promise you if you post the sales numbers on the board, your sales will increase."

He said, "I'm not sure."

I was so positive it would work I went to the owner of the company and pleaded my case. When he heard what it did at the last employer I worked with, he said "we'll try it!"

To make a long story short, sales increased 20% the following month and stayed higher on average from the previous year. And I wasn't surprised when I found out the sales rep had lied to me about his production.

So, the point is, the fit doesn't need to be perfect. Internal competition is fine, almost necessary.

6.Q: *Tell me about a time when you were satisfied with how your compensation was structured. How was it structured? Why did you like it?*

Decide now if he's going to like your compensation program and can adapt to it. I would only share it with him at this point if he's seasoned, and you need it to sell him on the opportunity.

If you've made points here, schedule the face-to-face interview.

This process is about subtle selling and you've piqued his interest. Don't oversell it, just close on the interview. Then figure how to get him into the fold.

Many people say not to discuss compensation on the first interview. That may be true for the candidate, but for the business owner or hiring manager, it's ok to discuss ranges so a top performer can know the potential. Top sales performers want unlimited opportunity.

If you try to cap that, you won't get high achievers. Either that or your business will plateau at a certain level. At that time you may want a sales-process expert review of your methodologies.

7. Q: Skill set questions can be utilized here to confirm they have sold the desired products or to the right buyers and have earned substantial commissions. I also ask what they've earned over the phone because history usually dictates their future potential. If they are way out of your price range, it's better to know now.

Keep this scorecard by the phone and keep track of their answers
Give them one point for each yes. If they score under 7 don't see them.

                                                                Yes   No

1. Are they enthusiastic about your opportunity?
2. Do they seem smooth and prepared to ask questions?
3. Would I let them schedule an appointment with me if I was a prospect of my company?
4. Did I feel that they were sincere during the discussion?
5. Am I looking forward to meeting with them?
6. Did they close by asking for an interview?
7. Are they confident/comfortable with themselves?
8. Are they asking about opportunity at your company?

9. Were they good listeners by not making you repeat yourself?
10. Did they sound persuasive?
11. How did you feel when you put down the phone? Were you smiling?

TOTAL

Remember 7 or
under, goodbye.

FIRST INTERVIEW QUESTIONS

Use as many questions as you need but make certain this interview gains enough information to make a qualified decision.

Recently I heard about a local company hiring an out of town search firm (must be experts?) and they were doing group interviews for hiring sales people. The only situation I know of in which this method may work is in entry-level sales, where reps might be prospecting as a team. Frankly, I don't think it has potential in professional sales organizations.

How does a sales rep feel being one of 20 in a room? Creative? Independent? Select? Is this person supposed to be important to your organization? It wouldn't feel special to me if I were interviewed that way. No, those recruiters should be selling macramé on South Beach (and probably will be soon).

And the company would be trying to develop loyalty? Judge individuality? Most top sales performers have some ego attached and want to be recognized for their contribution.

When a company starts a relationship with team interviews, it sets the stage for disloyalty, mistrust, and turnover because it's an "I don't care about you individually" approach.

Enough said about that. Now, on to the questions.

Q 1. Why do you want to work for this company? Or, why are you interviewing with me today?

One right answer could be "I don't know yet. It depends on

what you tell me, like what you're like to work for, and the many questions I have to ask. I'd like to learn about your products or services and understand the direction you're moving in."

Also, it's possible to discuss earning potential in a first interview if it's a sales position, but not particulars of an offer. There's no sense bringing someone back for a second interview if they can't earn what they need.

The key at this stage is to gauge if culture is a match and personalities fit. Candidate questions should be more about what the position entails and what daily activities are necessary to obtain goals. Questions like, who do I work with, and what is their background are also fine. And how can I move upward or grow from this position?

Q 2. Have your read our promotional materials and website? If yes, then... What interested you most there?

If the candidate HAS NOT reviewed the site or your marketing materials AND they did not get a 9 or 10 on your phone interview, end the interview. Wish them the best and say good-bye. You've saved some time.

Salespeople are normally excitable. They are most excitable in the beginning of a relationship. If they aren't interested enough to find out more, it's beneficial to find out now. YOU SHOULD THANK THEM because they saved you time. You saved resources to train, those "where's the orders?" type meetings and false expectations of potential business.

Q 3. Why did you leave your former companies? How would you evaluate them?

Go through each one and get real answers. Do they shuffle in their seat when you ask this question? Scrutinize answers like "I didn't like my boss" or "They overlooked me for a promotion".

One acceptable answer can be "They changed the commissions schedule and I couldn't earn what we originally discussed on the interview".

Now why is this a right answer? Because sales people tend to be similar to independent agents even though you've made them employees. They see themselves as owners of their time and talents. If the deal changes, many sales stars will leave and go to greener pastures. Many business owners would like to hear, "I stayed even though they cut my commissions because I liked the company and wanted to help when business slowed." Great answer. I have hired reps with both responses.

Now, SALES MANAGERS are often thought of differently. This is a person you've made a commitment to and vice-versa. They are someone who should, more often than not, ride the waves with you through bumps in the road.

Q 4. What was your quota at your last company and what was your percentage of attainment?

Of course, The McCandlish Group always gathers this information before we've spent time on a candidate. You may ask how others did with goal attainment in their organization and how they compared.

As they are explaining, if they didn't hit quota, they will say why. Remember the excuses because they will repeat those stories when they don't hit goal for your company.

By the way, I am always amazed at being told by former sales reps of dot-com start-ups that they didn't have a set quota. They just "tried to sell all they could". I heard it so often, it had to be partly factual. No wonder they went out of business in droves. No set numbers to shoot for each month is like driving blindly with no road map.

Q 5. How and why did you go into sales?

You're looking for honest answers here. Don't be critical if they say, "I love the short hours and big paychecks". Or they could say, "I like people and I've always been persuasive." In my case, I could have said, "I have an authority complex and I always out-sell everyone to keep people off my back, have a flexible schedule and take time off when I want it."

How would you respond to that one? Be ready for anything here. Not many wrong answers but you'll gain understanding of the individual before and after hiring.

Q 6. What do your best friends do?

A motivational speaker once said you will earn approximately what your 10 best friends earn.

I like this because it tells me where he/she is socially. Usually sales pros know many others. Also, if he runs with the country club gang, he's possibly a golfer who wants to earn more and "keep up" with friends......oh, and play some golf. Be careful of golf-aholics. If he networks that way, I'm fine with that. BUT, I don't like playing golf when there's real prospecting to be done.

Now, if they cut out early to play golf, are motivated by it, AND make quota just to have flexible hours and play when they want, I'M OK WITH THAT TOO! As competitive as business is these days, it's hard to make quota and keep a 2 handicap.

Q 7. Describe your sales training to me.

Big company is good. Smaller sales organization is also ok. Did they learn to hunt? Even if they aren't in a hunter's role, it's a good knowledge base.

Q 8. Do you work better in an unstructured environment or structured?

Now savvy reps know that most small businesses are unstructured. And to many that's the appeal. Many sales pros don't like to be managed daily as the original draw to a sales career was the freedom.

However, many people know if they are better producers with regular meetings, weekly or daily reporting, and managers to brainstorm with. This information will help you manage and support the rep.

Q 9. What are your personal interests or hobbies?

You be the judge but some companies don't particular like the "bar" hobbies....darts, etc. If all their hobbies are around alcohol related activities, you could have a potential problem. If they say they lift weights, run, play tennis or golf to relieve stress and enjoy life, great. If they are soccer Dads and Moms, even better. Some people make a habit of networking in Chamber of Commerce events as a habit. I love those work-aholics. For a sales hire, they're usually the best of "holics". Balance may be great but working all day and night makes a better bottom line. Sorry for being honest. Also, be careful of the skydivers.....?

Q 10. Where did you stand amongst the total sales forces in your last position?

Get a feel for where they were. Sometimes even top 25% is fine because of the many potential mismatches for culture, mismanagement, bad products etc. Top 10% is very good. When an AE says they were in the top 5% or even top 2% ask more specific questions. You may need to shorten your process a bit with those candidates and get them on board. Be careful not to shorten it too much but let them know they are special. You may start selling the benefits of your company to them a little faster than normal. Every sales executive is not created equal. Stars perform to get special attention.

Q 11. Are you comfortable in companies that publish sales numbers internally for employees to see?

This will tell you if they are competitive or not. Non-competitive sales people concern me.

Q 12. What other kinds of opportunities are you interviewing for? With what companies?

This is important because if they are not looking for other sales jobs, you need to ask why? Why sell for our company and not others? I normally would not hire a sales rep that is looking for a project manager's slot, a GM position or anything else but sales. The what companies question tells you what size and type of company they are drawn to.

Q 13. Ever been arrested or convicted of anything?

Use your own judgment here. I'm soft on credit related issues but criminal is something else. What can you live with? If it's drinking and driving, are they still drinking? Are you at risk?

Q 14. What are you trying to earn in the next twelve months? (Not what would you like them to make)

If they want 75k and you want reps to earn 90k then say goodbye because they're underachievers. If they want 150k, consider if that's realistic. They should feed it back to you. Be honest.

If you like their answers, tell them about your opportunity. Tell them how the company was started, and hopefully they will ask.

It's ok to mention upward mobility and where they go next unless the position is virtually unlimited with upwards of 100k to earn. Also discuss how they can earn more each year by representing your company. They can add more accounts, add more products and services, improve in ability, add more responsibilities, etc.

You can end the interview with "I'd like to review this information and I'll contact you to discuss a second meeting."

Or, you can say, "I have other candidates and I'd like to give this consideration before I ask you back for a second interview. As I mentioned earlier, we always do two interviews. Are you still ok with that process? Great! Thanks for seeing me today."

If they are interested, and they are a salesperson, they will probably respond in the positive. Some will try to get an understanding of where they compare with the other candidates. If not and they don't ask or hint they are interested, it's probably not a good match. The total time spent here should not be more than an hour to an hour and a half if you like them. You can cut them off whenever you're getting answers you don't like and send them away. Time is important. Learn to use the broom! GO to the next with authority. You're looking for someone to make your decision easy. THE RIGHT CANDIDATE IS AN EASY DECISION TO MAKE! IF YOU'RE AGONIZING OVER A SALES HIRE, PASS.

Sometimes making decisions like this without help is challenging. Qualified sales recruiters can advise you, but if you don't have a budget for that service, solicit help from current employees like the receptionist. Ask her to evaluate demeanor, manners, and anything she'd like to offer. It keeps them involved and gives you another perspective.

Always ask "Would you buy our product from that person? If no, make them tell you specifically why.

The only advice I have at the end of the first interview is do you like them better or worse than after your phone interview? WHY? Once you determine that decide whether to bring them in for a last interview or not. At this time you should be fairly certain of their ability to do the job, and soon decide if you want to work with them.

THE SECOND INTERVIEW

The second interview includes more specific and measurable questions.

Please get another person's opinion of the candidate during the process. Some companies report success with having the candidate ride with the sales manager in the field for a day or half day. This is effective because you can see how the candidate interacts with customers and you'll get to know them before you commit.

1. What does your present (or last) employer think of your work there?

If they say, "I've created enough business there to make it profitable for them to keep me" then they're thinking about the bottom line and that's OK.

If they say, "Oh, I don't care what they think because they were blankety blank blank and didn't know what they were doing anyway" then you have to dig deeper. Ask why they respond in that manner.

Do you know the company they were with? Were they actually as bad as the candidate says? They could be. Some companies are known for discrepancies around paying sales commissions.

JUST BECAUSE SOMEONE HAS PUT OUT A SHINGLE AND STARTED A BUSINESS DOESN'T MEAN THEY ARE REPUTABLE. Actually it can mean no one would hire them. Bad-mouthing is not good, but do some research before you dismiss a candidate who might have been honest in their assessment.

Just find out why and determine the validity of the remark. They may just be guilty of not doing more initial homework on the employer previous to interviewing.

2. What was your best sales accomplishment?

They should have a story or two ready because if they are accomplished at all they have told the story before. Actually, top sellers have many stories and that's why they are top sellers. People love stories.

3. Any of your sales activity that hasn't been well received by your present employer?

Maybe a deal they gave away or made a bidding mistake on? Back in my office equipment sales days, it was common practice to discount a copier to hit a certain level of points total for the month. The company and I both profited but since the total put me in a higher pay bracket, I earned more on all the deals I sold that month. SO it made sense to occasionally discount that one and go on.

4. What talents do you have that match well with our firm?

5. What is the best working environment for you?

6. Tell me about a time you were in a meeting and someone said something inaccurate. What did you do?

A good answer is raising their hand for clarification to ask are you certain?"

7. How can you improve yourself?

It's a better way to say, "what are your weaknesses?" Everyone knows they can improve but won't always say what their weaknesses are.

8. How often do you have meetings at your present, or last company?

The question will make them think on their feet and you'll gain information about other companies' styles and direction. Maybe this candidate needs more meetings than you provide so you should address how they will be managed.

9. Describe the most productive meeting you've participated in recently. What made it productive and what was your role?

10. Tell me about a meeting you've attended that was unproductive and why it was. What was your role? The key here is their participation.

11. Have you ever had to make a client satisfied by making an unrealistic or difficult commitment? Did the company ever not support you and what was the situation?

If the sales person didn't have a situation like that, it's ok. If they were very productive they could have made promises regularly and are no longer employed because the company didn't want to keep losing money on their commitments. Back to office equipment sales, I often gave away paper and a copier stand to make a deal happen in my time frame rather than wait on the decision maker to drag it out and possibly lose the sale. We had giveaways built into our point system and I paid some small wholesale amount. It was a smart sales tool.

As they interview more, you'll find out how you compare against other companies who do not have good sales systems in place.

12. Describe an organizational change at your old employer and explain how that affected your team and your personal productivity?

Some AE's cannot get motivated or change course after a change in organization. Everything changes and good reps understand profitable business. If you aren't changing things semi-regularly, you'll get bitten. Continue to fine tune and grow and good sales reps will adjust.

13. Most AE's have had to deal with a difficult person occasionally. Give me an example of a difficult customer and how you negotiated with them.

14. Describe a situation when you were trying to do many things at the same time. How did you handle it?

Did they convince others to assist? Did they try to do it alone? This demonstrates degree of persuasiveness.

15. How did you plan last week's daily work activities? What activities do you plan and when do you do that?

Do they plan on their own time? Not necessary, but an attractive trait.

16. What are important measurable sales statistics you monitor as part of your planning?

Important to know how motivated they are and how detail-oriented. What is their closing average? Do they know it?

17. What objectives have you set for yourself for the year? For the month? For the week? For the day?

If you ask like that, you will know if they are keepers or not. They may show embarrassment if they don't plan. Few plan weekly but monthly is more popular.

Remember, companies that drive numbers and have daily sales reporting systems grow faster as a rule. Technology-based companies have longer sales cycles but need to monitor activities in terms of presentations, phone calls, appointments, and product trials.

18. Describe a sales contest that you lost and your friends and associates knew you wanted to win. How did you respond?

They may say, I've never lost a sales contest. Then your decision is "do they need to be motivated through sales contests?" or "Can I drive sales in the manner this rep is accustomed? Can we keep this candidate motivated?"

19. At any point in your career have you wondered if you chose the right career for yourself? When? What did you do?

Even top salespeople tell me they would've liked to become a movie star, radio announcer, sports figure, doctor, etc. This doesn't change because you're in sales. There are days, of course, after a certain amount of rejection when we all want to think about another (easier) product to sell with fat commissions and many days off in a row. Who doesn't?

It's great if they say, I just enjoy selling, and I'll always be selling.

20. Have you received criticism from your manager lately? How did it make you feel?

See if they are resilient. They could say, "I had it coming but it didn't taste good."

Or, they could blame the manager's style...."I didn't like the fact he said this when he didn't say it to so and so." Remember whom they blame.

21. Describe a situation in which you wish you had acted differently with someone at work?

22. Tell me about a customer you won that took a long time.

Tell me about one you persisted with and didn't win.

Look for work ethic, not closing average here.

Listen for number of attempts, if they changed their approach, gave the client something new to think about or was it crude insistence and repetitive?

23. What were the biggest obstacles you had to overcome to get to where you are today?

24. What were the most stressful activities of your last position?

25. In your present position how do you define doing a good job? Are you?

26. Describe a time you made annual quota and a time you didn't.

27. Tell me about the three most important people in your work experiences who influenced you most.

28. What has been the biggest contribution you've made to the organization?

29. What are your career objectives and how are you doing so far towards achieving them?

30. Have you ever done any public speaking? Tell me about it.

31. How often have you followed up, as a percentage, after the service or product you sold was delivered?

This is good information. I'd like to know, how often they followed up without having to be told. If they assumed the company did a good job of support, that's great. But it's a mindless, careless salesperson that doesn't follow up, if for no other reason than asking for referrals.

If they seldom followed up, they probably won't admit it. If they were extremely productive still, then they are mechanical, robotic, and can still be productive in a sales capacity because they do the numbers. They are less likely to be good managers because as a rule, sales managers care about people and are drawn to management and mentoring. Sales managers insensitive to human needs turnover sales staff and cost you.

32. What are the longest hours you've ever had to work at _____? How many hours do you normally work?

Now is the best time to explore this and to talk about what the top people in your organization usually do for schedules. If you need them 50 hours a week, tell them.

There you have it, choose all or few of these questions but I'd ask at least 15-20 to get a feel for their interest, motivation, and fit. Notice I don't say talent? It's because sales is a career where a new job may get someone excited about opportunity and they may exceed everything they've done in the past.

Has your child thrived in a new classroom with a new teacher? Is he doing better with a woman teacher now or possibly vice-versa? Maybe someone with a new teaching style? Is he better with teachers who write instruction or those who read it?

Dynamics change with venue. A great coach can motivate his team to the Super Bowl and changing sales managers can also have a major impact on sales candidates.

Now, you may not need all of these questions but I'd say choose the ones most appealing to your situation. Don't cheat yourself by not asking many questions and letting sales pros take over the interview. You need information to make a decision. If you get wowed at their communication abilities you'll be distressed you didn't explore key issues later.

Then, HIT THE GROUND RUNNING... TRAIN THEM!

It is absolutely futile to run ads, hire salespeople (or headhunters), and make an effort to bring in top talent if you do not have an immediate, fast-start training program on your product or services. It should include who, where, when, why and how of selling your stuff! A quick start incentive to produce sales should be stated as part of the program.

Urgency is communicated immediately and if the new representative doesn't respond to the training and sales spiff then you better call in your guarantee with the recruiter or keep your newspaper ad running. You'll be replacing them soon.

Have a knowledgeable product person assist in teaching with a few experts from your company. Those experts can give their "two cents", build a relationship of their own with the sales team member, and the new sales person will have a better understanding of what makes the technical side of the business work.

This practice will help establish their relationships with others and break up the monotony of one trainer. Then when they don't sell it right, the product expert doesn't confront them emotionally because they have a relationship. Just like the construction supervisor who is trying to educate new home salespeople on construction materials. The sales representative promised a 4-month delivery to the new homeowners and the construction guy flips because of weather problems and says, "Don't do that, ever. We can never promise a drop-dead delivery date. We can't control the weather."

Now the sales person knows it's almost impossible to sell the home when they can't give an approximate time for delivery.

So, the situation needs a manager's involvement. A realistic goal should be set by management and agreed upon with the sales representative. The production people have to understand deadlines and salespeople must understand not to promise what can't be delivered.

Companies that have a proactive training program that addresses issues like these can reduce sales turnover by putting everything in writing. At least it's a starting point. Then they need to discuss these issues with all involved. When sales and production are working together it's a beautiful thing!

INTERVIEW QUESTIONS FOR SALES MANAGERS

These are usually asked on a second interview as the first interview questions can be combined with these to complete the process.

Q1. What do previous sales teams you managed say about you?

This is an easy question for them to brag about past accomplishments and open up to more.

Q2. What would the previous companies say about your ability to hire, train, manage, and drive numbers for the enterprise?

This is a critical question but candidates will open up and tell you about times when they disagreed with management and why this or that didn't result in quota. Keep probing and you'll get answers here. Whether you buy into it or not is questionable.

What could they say that is credible? The TRUTH. Is what they are telling you sincere and verifiable? Jot it down, and then check it out with their references. Absolute qualities of a sales manager include honesty, trustworthiness, patience to teach, and holding others accountable for activities and results.

Q3. Do any of your previous hires credit you for training and assisting them in their development to star status? How did you develop them?

Tell me about one or two. What are their names and phone

numbers?

Again, make notes and check it out. If you can't ask these difficult questions now, you'll be challenged to manage a savvy sales manager.

These types of references will not say much negative but historically will open up more than traditional references. I explain later how to pull information from them.

Q 4. How did you handle underachievers?

Did he replace them quickly? Did he have a system in place, maybe two months in a row off quota and they are gone to that next great opportunity in the sky? What was his policy? Did he work with them first to see if the company was being fair with them? For instance, some companies have territories that are undeveloped with no accounts and hire a new sales representative hoping he will "go get'em" and establish the territory. When someone is new to a sales position they normally throw energy at the position and can open new business through enthusiasm alone.

Companies often hire reps on straight commission and ask for results that take longer than expected to develop. If they don't make it the company has limited exposure except for their time. I know of many companies that have been built on salespeople's "backs". It just seems to be part of the deal.

Q 5. What motivates you about this job?

You should see him get a little excited if he's already aware of the opportunity and potential. If not he should fake it. And he should answer immediately unless he needs to clarify something like, "Did you say I'll have P&L responsibility and make marketing decisions that impact my bottom line? No hesitation here. Now some managers don't really show emotion but are still effective. I prefer the ones that are animated because people around them get excited.

Q 6. What annoys you about this job?

(Important) This issue could get bigger as time passes. Make sure it's not insurmountable at this stage.

Q 7. Did you ever go against company policy or procedure and why?

Often sales stars will make promises that are hard to keep. Remember that it's usually the producers who are being creative and trying to bring "something" to the table. They are scrambling to not lose a potential sale by asking their company to bend rules or throw in this or that to make the sale. Often the sale can't be made and it's time to move on, but you want to hear about all the decisions being made in your territory.

Now, I'd want my reps to get us in on every deal possible and have an opportunity to bid or compete for the business. Don't blame the reps always fighting to make a deal happen when the passive ones seldom get that far. No Problems, No Issues... No Sales.

Q 8. Were you involved in strategy at your last position?

Important to know so you can decide if you need a strategy guy or an implementer. If you want a robot to carry out the company plan and not question it, that's OK. Just make sure the candidate is on that track.

Q 9. Did you ever feel strongly that the company you represented was going in the wrong direction with product development or marketing or sales direction? What did you do?

Should give you an idea of their independence. If they knew the direction was questionable and didn't say something, I'd be concerned.

Q 10. Ever been asked to do something you felt was unethical by an employer?

Like, use your relationship for purchasing decisions you knew was wrong for the customer? Like the mechanic who recommended a new water pump when yours worked fine?

Q 11. Tell me about someone to whom you offered feedback for improvement and they resisted or disagreed. How did you handle that?

One right answer could be "In my mind I evaluated whether I said it improperly, at the wrong time when others heard, or communicated indirectly so as to confuse. When I decided it should've been clear I asked for a private meeting with the individual and said, "Why are you resisting my direction? It is my position to direct this team and give feedback based on your performance. If you were performing and making goal, I wouldn't have commented."

Q 12. Discuss your plan for top performers. Do you have a different plan for each team member or one for all? Did you develop it with or without the performer's involvement?

A minimum acceptable standard by which all must perform is best. From there, the gifted ones get individual attention and together we set goals that are custom made for their talents. Stars need higher goals to achieve or they become bored and look for new challenges. You should constantly ask for more from your stars and not spend much time with the lower third of your team. Replace them and spend more time on your mid and upper thirds. When you cut from the bottom, the rest perform better without even a conversation. Funny how that happens!!!

C'mon Mike, don't be so cold-blooded. Cold blooded you say?

Most sales teams need pushed, shoved, and managed. Few are actually self-motivated to do the job daily. The ones that NEED to work usually do. Need and fear are great motivators; something to consider in your hiring process.

Q 13. Tell me how you trained new employees? What is their week-by-week activity?

Q 14. How do you utilize direct reports to maximize performance?

Sales people dislike activity reports but companies that make them part of the regimen have better control. It's the method to receive information from the field. Activity reporting is a constant struggle but it probably won't change unless you have some way to tie in their paychecks with the information. If you have creative ways to receive them from sales people please email me your ideas. Some companies do actually tie the reports to their compensation. It's a part of the offer letter.

One of the best sales managers I knew went over the activity report, asked about last week's appointments and when I said, "the customer said they wanted me to call back later," he did. He would contact them right then and introduce himself. He would ask if they had enough information to make a logical decision and offer his phone number if they couldn't reach me. He then asked the reason they weren't buying and often created a closing opportunity over the phone. By the way, shame on me if I told him I saw someone and I didn't. This method ensured there was no creative writing happening on those reports.

Q 15. Have your sales teams always agreed with the numbers corporate has set for them to achieve? If not, what did you do?

"I received their buy-in" is a good answer. They bought in after a great planning meeting. If I couldn't sell them I may have to replace them. I got each one's commitment in a room where we all discussed possibilities. I was prepared with appropriate information, which gave me an advantage.

Q 16. How do you normally handle the stars that don't need much management but consistently sell over goal and way above? How do you keep them interested and motivated to set higher goals and keep them "on the team?"

A good response is "I communicated to my stars, became their friend, met for lunch, and supported their efforts. If others saw it as preferential they needed to step up their game to be included. If you do more, you get more in sales. It's a results business and stars should be treated as such. This doesn't mean throw more money at them. It means using them as examples. Brag on them in public. Let them talk in meetings and share their methods. Give them meetings to do and watch them grow because they've accepted a share of the enterprises welfare."

Three management styles seem to be
1. SELL THEM
2. TELL THEM
3. MAKE THEM

We all know making them doesn't work so START SELLING!!! The owner usually is the most persuasive person in the organization.

You can give sales stars new responsibilities. Let them develop a new territory, accounts, or even new markets and new products.

We could devote a chapter to managing stars. First, forget the antiquated business model of "We're the boss and you must go sell, that's your job." That mentality doesn't work well with stars. It will with "robots" that do everything you ask because it's their job, but not the stars. The stars go elsewhere because "they can". Developing Stars could be my next book.

Look what Phil Jackson of the Los Angeles Lakers accomplished with his stars. He doesn't seem to lose them to other teams because he created challenges for them to do more than they thought possible.

If you consistently lose your stars you better have an endless supply of new talent or a great training program. Good luck. It's hard to grow if you're losing key talent to competitors or creating competitors by limiting their growth because they don't continue to fit your business model. Update it, be open to changing it, and grow.

Q 17. How would you handle this problem?

Give the prospective manager a case study to think through and give you feedback. The problem should be whatever issues you're having in your business. When he communicates to you, consider his answer plus additional aspects. How did he arrive at his/her conclusion? What was his/her thinking process? Does he/she understand the business and did the analysis consider issues important to the decision?

Great sales managers are the backbone of corporate America. They are smart, capable sales people in their own right, normally with a good work ethic, and have chosen to share their talents and sales secrets with others for mutual benefit. The good ones don't say, "wish I wouldn't have spent so much time on that guy"...they know not everyone takes the coaching this time but may get it on the next go around.

There is nothing as satisfying as someone calling you out of the blue, years later and saying, "Thanks, I remember what you taught me and I had a great year using it." It just feels good.

REFERENCES

Let's discuss them in direct terms called L I T I G A T I O N S.

Companies now are afraid to give any information other than dates of employment and sometimes the title or job description of the candidate. They cannot say, "John Doe wasn't very productive here" for fear of being sued.

Since the minimal information offered doesn't help other than to determine truthfulness on the resume, The McCandlish Group asks the candidate for work-related references. Some give three, some send ten. The more the merrier because you can cross-reference and by asking the right questions, find out more than the candidate thinks will be offered.

Additionally, we have found that hiring managers are sometimes overly skeptical about the information contained in Candidate Reference Reports. There is often the perception that a candidate can somehow skew or game what is being said by their references. It has been our experience that if we speak with three or more listed reference contacts provided by the candidate and ask open ended questions in a friendly manner about the candidate's personal character, the nature of their working relationship, examples of problem definition and solving, ability to drive change, etc., a valid picture of the candidate's preferred work style and true ability to get things done –DOES IN FACT EMERGE.

We like to then compare these findings with what is presented on the candidate's resume or what we have heard from the candidate during the interview process. The story about the candidate that emerges from this cross checking process does represent information that is highly reliable and helpful in painting a clear picture that is often predictive of how the candidate will behave and, ultimately, perform in their new job. A solid reference check is a reason for The McCandlish Group's strong hired candidate track record ---and of course high client and candidate satisfaction ratings.

ISSUES OF AGE

Most hiring managers would not have a problem with age. Age gives us experience and, when asked, most hiring managers understand mature candidates give you better service in the following situations:

Strategy

Reliability

Credibility

Responsibility

What most sales hiring managers look for is the following:

Energy

Fresh ideas

Long hours-productivity

Results

Sales managers can be older, young bloods usually are a better find for territories and hunting.

The December 2nd, 2003 Wall Street Journal featured an article, <u>Aged to Perfection?</u> More Companies Seek Older Leaders describes several recent "headline-worthy" CEO departures where "old" leaders are being tapped to fill their shoes. At first glance the headline gives the reader hope that businesses are valuing wisdom gained with age and proven track records. However, the article reveals that many of our leading corporations are desperate for leadership because they haven't been smart in developing leaders and succession plans.

Is age discussed with headhunters? Of course it is. We have to know every requirement or we waste our time. We've already discussed that time is money for the client and ourselves. If the client doesn't give us complete requirements and we don't ask, we're at fault.

In key VP Sales or Marketing roles, I'm usually more comfortable with variety of experiences than someone freshly out of a large company. I need proof that they can manage in the confines a small business without marketing strategists and administrators.

By comparison, it's easier for a young MBA at Motorola to do a great job managing a division, grow it 15% and crowned to be a "superachiever" at their annual award ceremony than to move along a start-up with limited resources. I like to see success at that level in addition to a Motorola experience, and then you have something.

Sure, a young manager with a 10 to 12 year run with a big company and continuous responsibilities must be considered as a viable candidate for a small firm to utilize. All I'm really saying is the experienced manager with both experiences is far less risk. I'd also rather see 5 to 7 years at one firm unless they have had a fast career path with solid promotions.

I also tend to favor the entrepreneurial managers who have start-up experience and have started with no sales and driven to 5 million or more. Or taken a loser and turned it around within 12 months by hitting the pavement, providing strategy and implementing it. They have installed proper sales methodologies, employed strategic sales strategies, and shown spending discipline when it started rolling.

MISCELLANEOUS ISSUES OF HIRING

Did the candidate have too many previous jobs?

Sales candidates can move around easier than other careers because "selling" is their expertise and they are their own product. They know how to push the right buttons, interview, and say the right things to get hired. Even if they've had a new job every two years for ten years, there's someone out there to take a chance on them, especially with a verified history of quick results at every stop. When you have an open territory and a live body who's spouting great things about their past, it's tempting to take them up on it. Just do their references.

Look beyond the amount of changes a sales representative has made and understand the reasons. There are legitimate reasons to change employers.

Of course many will say,

"The candidate made poor choices .....must be a poor sales person."

I'm not sure how that equates. Sales people don't have to be brain surgeons. They are known to be relationship business developers, not CEO's. The CEO can take the credit or the heat for decisions. The sales person sometimes is not a great decision maker.

So should it matter that in the late 1990's they went for a couple start-ups that could have made them rich overnight. Their present company cut their territory, made poor decisions on their own (like many dot-coms who misspent the money) and the sales person struck out on their own. I don't have a problem with that.

It was more a sign of the times and adjusting to the market.

TOO MANY PREVIOUS JOBS BUT YOU LIKE THEM ANYWAY?

You must decide if the reasons are legitimate. Again, for example, in the late 90's it was easy to get recruited or sold on moving out. It was very tempting to "go for it" when a recruiter called with hopes of getting rich in a tech start-up. When you know you can survive by selling your way into another job and you're in a mediocre, no growth opportunity, it seems an easy decision. Because of that unique time period, I wouldn't penalize those job seekers for taking a high-risk opportunity. Some stories found sales reps getting large amounts of stock through work equity and actually accumulating large nest eggs for future investments or early retirement. Of course there are more stories of failure, but no risk, no reward. I might have gone for one of those opportunities myself, BUT NO ONE CALLED ME!

If you take the challenge to continuously improve your business to provide good opportunities for sales people, you'll stay ahead of your competitors. You may not like the reason you're making improvements but look at the sales rep like he's the customer.

Is the salesperson financed properly to wait through the ramp time before they start earning a higher income?

Depending on the sales cycle, many new reps come in "under-financed" and need a draw or advance soon after hire. This is a frequent issue in draw versus commission opportunities. Just have a plan on how to deal with those requests. A $200 million consulting company had 20% of their sales team on an advance schedule because commissions were inconsistent. Most companies don't have this practice available to them but some companies believe an advance commissions policy is necessary for their growth. Software companies normally have an advance commissions method in place because of the long sales cycle.

If you were looking for an opinion, I'd say some reps might be worth coddling in the beginning and "financing" if your upside with them is good. Each rep has to be evaluated individually. The consulting company I spoke of had tremendous turnover and had to hire 25 new sales reps to keep three for six months. The company sold services with a very high margin so they justified advancing dollars to sales representatives because of their tremendous growth. The owner called it a cost of doing business in his industry.

Consulting experience on the resume.

Sometimes when hiring managers review individuals who went into consulting on their own, it's a red flag. It can mean they don't want to be managed, feel their skills set is above the rest, and probably had a problem integrating within the organization. Somewhere along the line they started their own business.

Although technology has spurred some interesting dynamics in this area, hiring managers in most industries are concerned about hiring independent consultants as employees. It does seem to be "older thinking" though.

Technology professionals often get better mileage from consultants than employees. They see consultants as entrepreneurial, up to date on industry trends, and more knowledgeable of how market leaders are doing it.

If consultants can get enough work, they are fine. Just know many managers see it as a non-work experience. They don't see them as a fit where an employee may still be more manageable, although this approach is short-sided.

Often when someone has gone into consulting, real employment opportunities haven't been available to them. And why not consult if the pay is more than an employee situation earns? Business owners should certainly understand that mentality.

It's the same as theirs. The usual concern is the consultant will take off on them after being trained or even take employees or clients with them.

Partially, it represents a decision that was short lived because they saw an opportunity to work fewer hours and earn more. It's the American way but if it doesn't work long term, the consultant is seen as someone who would probably do it again. Then, where is the employer but searching for another employee?

Hiring consultants is like hiring entrepreneurs in that they don't always fit a corporate structure and won't stick around if a better opportunity presents itself. Sometimes the opportunity is from one of your customers or your employees that they connect with to start the next venture.

Now, don't be afraid to grow by not hiring a consultant, just be selective and know the possible outcome.

But the salesperson has changed industries many times

This can mean many things. Maybe when their chosen industry went soft, as all do, they weren't "financed" properly for down times. So, because they could, they changed industries to a hotter product or service. In general terms the sales pro can easily change industries better than any other discipline. Sales and finance skill sets aren't as industry specific and can change industries easier than others.

Product knowledge is always important for a competitive advantage but selling ability is more important to hire for than product knowledge.

The down side for the salesperson is if they were away from a given industry for awhile they weren't privileged to industry trends and recent changes or new technology relative to that industry. They can usually catch up quickly.

Unemployment or long layoffs

When a true sales person has been unemployed for a while, I have to question their motivation and need. The general reasons to be totally off work are either health related or they have enough cash reserves. If they have worked hard, made good decisions and generated lots of cash, then employers should not be overly skeptical of a layoff. But, since the best sales pros can always find something to sell, unless they fall into the category of these scenarios, I'd question a long layoff.

If they were burned out and took some time off, that would also adversely affect a decision to bring them in. An exception would be made if they had participated in the sale of an equity venture and took time to shop for a good opportunity.

It's a better scenario for the candidate to have choices than working because of the money. Conversely, when sales reps work for you and need money, they seem to stay motivated for that reason. Many business owners prefer their sales reps broke and dependent upon them.

Here's a difficult situation. When I was selling outplacement services, I interviewed a man who stayed home for two years to raise the kids. His wife had a high-level management position. He wanted to re-enter the job market but needed some good ideas. Now, if we were all independent thinkers, would you hire this person if all things are equal or would you question why he stayed home and his wife brought home the bacon?

I have no problem saying it's ok for the wife to earn money for the family instead of the old stereotype of man being wage earner.

But, what happens when he wants to re-enter the market?

I told him to take something on a lower compensation level than he might have two years ago to get back into the workforce.

By being away from it all he missed out on present trends in his industry and was behind his competitors for the same positions he normally might have gotten. He could catch up soon if he was a producer and if not, he could consider an industry change.

Watch the candidate's career path. Is the timing right for them to achieve in your position? You can sometimes find a great sales pro who has been down because of poor career and life decisions and you get a feeling they need some help getting back on their feet. Often someone who needs to get re-established will do so and you may benefit. They may help grow your base and if they don't work out long term, a different type of sales person may then take over. And there's always a chance the sales rep will "find a home" since your environment and opportunity has helped them come back. Timing is everything.

You'll often need to look beyond the resume, as many sales types do not write an all-inclusive resume. VP Sales or Director level and above should have a well-written resume. But, sales executives don't always feel they need one because they feel past accomplishments should tell the story. Always ask for previous quota/goal and what their percentage of attainment or level of accomplishment was against goal.

Mistruths on the resume

You've caught them and you know it. How do you handle it?
1. If it's a lie, don't consider them for employment.
2. What is their crime?
a. If they have omitted early employment experiences, I don't always hold it against them. ***
b. If they have omitted short-term (under three months) experiences as in holding two jobs at once but listing only one, I also don't hold it against them.
c. If they have omitted part time experiences, I don't eliminate them.
d. Do they bring up the experiences in the interview? That is

beneficial if they discuss another experience they've left off.

***Recruiters differ here. There are hard liners who say they want your complete history. I've found some excellent sales people who did not include every job. They needed cash flow and worked for friends or helped build a house between sales positions. Or even worked part time while building a territory and left off the part-time employment. I'm ok with that.

Also, a segment of candidates have an outplacement company (at a high price) market them into the marketplace. They do so for many reasons. They may want to relocate and it makes the transition more challenging. Or, they just want an executive service to assist on technique and interviewing skills. Also, some of those companies market the resume to various job openings that match the candidate's skill set.

Don't discount a candidate who has someone else write his or her resume or distributes it for a fee. It shows commitment and a desire to uncover as many opportunities as possible. Neither action should draw scrutiny.

DEFINE THY OPENING

Whether you're getting outside assistance for the search or not, write down what the requirements are for the position. This will help you see what kind of person makes sense for you right now. It's similar thinking to a business plan.

Also, how will others in the organization refer their friends, associates, and possibly vendors if you don't have something in writing?

A headhunter's requirements list will include the following:

1. What kind of sales person do you need?

Account Manager Maintain status quo, gain internal referral business, don't lose the base and keep contacts happy. An account manager is good at relationships, follow up and support.

Account Executive Hunter type, new business development, closer.

Do you really need a hunter? How much prospecting is in the position? This is a key factor because the "Hunter" will cost you more. They'll cost you more in terms of time spent with them and compensation.

Business Development Consultant Open new accounts, ensure profitability, handle account management with a support person, and often handle marketing, targeting, and runs territory like their own business.

2. How long has the territory been open? Why?

This is a key question. Many thoughts run through a recruiters mind. Has the hiring company set unrealistic standards for the position? Is their product or service sellable? Are they paying competitive compensation? The McCandlish Group sees an open territory and says why? We help analyze this and fill the opening. OR we often just fill the opening.

Major responsibilities of position. Quota or goal expectations. Are they involved in collecting receivables? (A possible mistake if they are) Education; is college a requirement? (Not always for sales positions) Travel? Car involved? Pay mileage? Personality? (just have one?)

3. Compensation. How much commission versus guarantee. Guarantee is salary or draw? Is it recoverable? How about relocation?

4. Companies to target (and not). Careful here. Normally, companies say "So and so has financed our growth and owns our stock. Don't recruit their people." But most say, "Go anywhere. Everyone takes our sales people, so why not?"

5. Manage staff?

6. Company selling points.

History of company, key people candidate will work with, status of company in market, and direction.

7. Specifics of work experience to draw from.

Normally recruiters find someone who has done what the client wants at least once and normally twice in their background and is currently working in the industry.

8. Nature and amount of travel.

Important, as many positions are turned down for the travel.

9. Relocation: what is your budget to bring someone in.

Their house, insurance and miscellaneous costs of temporary housing, closing costs, etc.

additional considerations

Will your new sales executive get a client base to sell to?

If a client base exists in the territory, the new AE should acquire it. They shouldn't have to prove themselves. If certain customers are held back as a carrot, resentments will follow. Don't hire someone you lack confidence in to send to clients unless you lack confidence in your hiring process, then I understand hesitancy. In that case, I'd work with the new hire closer than usual until I was comfortable with them.

INTERNET POSTINGS

Here are some hints on how to post openings since many of you will post your own

Use an Employee Value Proposition

Before you delve into the advertised position, first determine your Employee Value Proposition (EVP). A well-written EVP answers the question, "Why would good talent work for your company rather than the competition?" Create and constantly refine the EVP to stay updated with current position parameters and bring the reader from awareness to interest or even action.

Keep it organized

People scan rather than read. Computer screens are read 25% slower than printed materials. Don't mix requirements with job descriptions or make the copy look overwhelming. Use bullets, subheads and different type for clarity. Start off with something compelling, like your Employee Value Proposition, then talk about the position. Finally, you can mention requirements and response information.

Give useful information

People are on the Internet to get information. They're not interested in fluff, so be descriptive. For example, many postings start off like this: "We're a high-growth leader, looking for an ambitious, goal-oriented professional with the drive to make a difference." A lot of time was spent filling the sentence with meaningless adjectives rather than information that is meaningful to the candidate's decision making.

As I mentioned earlier, hiring is not "about the company". If you're a growth company, that's great. It means fast promotions and more opportunities. How about "Due to tremendous growth, industry leading software developer has immediate sales openings for self-starting professionals with great attitude and rolodex. Leverage your experience into a competitive salary, stock options and high sales commissions."

Remember WIIFM? (What's In It For Me)? This ad says there is opportunity for the right people.

Personalize the posting

Make the tone of your copy conversational. Forget "the candidate will" and other non-attractive phrases. Talk directly to the reader by using pronouns like "you." That sounds like you're talking to the reader, is easier to read, and lets the candidate mentally see them in the position.

Be action-oriented

Accelerate. Accomplish. Achieve. These action verbs help drive people from interest to action. How many times do you see postings with flat verbs like "this is a great opportunity" when they could be creating action with a phrase such as "seize this opportunity."

Use descriptive titles

Companies sometimes use internal job titles for postings, but some job titles do not resonate with readers. Don't use Account Coordinator when you need a Customer Service Representative. Using a title that is less accepted limits readership. For sites with a search results page put additional pertinent information in the title like information about the position or the company's advantages as an employer (like a commission or bonus or proprietary new product).

Finally, don't use company jargon in the title. That includes insider language only known to your current employees or position levels. Administrative Assistant II means nothing to the reader. Administrative Assistant is sufficient.

SALES POSITIONS

Many sales related positions are listed here. Remember that many companies call their revenue creating positions special names to make the consumer believe they are not sales people. Often, consultant fits this description.

For instance, in the management consulting industry, a services sales person will schedule an analysis of a client company to determine if the company has a cash flow, sales and marketing or possible an inventory control issue to fix. The person sent in to analyze is called a business analyst. This analyst knows the basics of business and how the company should operate. But, their main goal is to convince the business owner his business is upside down and to hire their firm to correct the problems before he is finally bankrupt or has mismanaged the company into the ground.

Companies have different names for revenue generators. The telemarketer that calls you is an outbound call center specialist. Their main and only goal is to book new or add on business. Why don't they just call them that and say sales representative? Because the phrase "sales representative" can be a negative connotation. It's right up there with "contract" instead of "agreement". Or, something you "sign" instead of "authorize". It's all semantics.

Tech companies know the systems engineer is supposed to be there to install new software but he's also looking for add-on sales. He can sell maintenance agreements and probably has a sales quota.

Here's the list.

Account Executive	Product marketing manager
National sales accounts manager	Senior account executive

Account representative
Contract administrator
Customer service representative
District sales manager
Relationship manager
Retail zone manager
Sales agent
Sales engineer
Systems engineer pre and post
Top call center executive
Territory manager
Direct sales manager, Banking
Insurance agent
Manufacturers representative
Senior marketing director

Channel sales rep
Call center representative
Retail sales manager
Retail zone manager
Retail store manager
Regional sales manager
Sales director
Sales trainer
Technical sales support I-IV
Top merchandising planner
Visual merchandiser, Director
Inside technical sales
International sales director
Marketing manager
Merchandising buyer planner

NEGOTIATING COMP PLANS

What is appropriate compensation in your industry?

If your comp plan is significantly different, explain it early in the interview, even mention it on the phone if it positions you favorably with the prospect. Remember, you're selling very subtly, but if the candidate has other companies courting them, you need to inform quickly and sound enthusiastic. Every sales candidate wants to be wanted. It's been communicated often by job seekers that being wanted is as important as money.

AND, although during interviews people say money isn't the sole deciding factor, for top salespeople, the potential of working in an environment of unlimited opportunity is essential.

Get advice from a professional before delivering an offer. They will give you some things to think about. In general terms, companies that hire at the VP level can and will do employment contracts.

You may have to be creative if you're competing for a proven CEO or VP of Sales candidate.

WORKING WITH RECRUITERS

Business Owners and hiring managers......why work with recruiters? (Never thought you'd ask)

1. When recruiters see a great candidate it's obvious! And we keep them on file.

We typically talk to 30 to 40 candidates a day. I often review or at least take a quick look at fifty to three hundred resumes in a day. So, when a star comes along, it's obvious and I often try to market that person to possible matches and keep them in our database.

This works in your favor if you've engaged a firm to do your search work. Getting the RIGHT candidate is everything. How do recruiters get the right candidate? They search, they recruit, they pull from another source, maybe someone who's not happy somewhere else and you offer a better fit. Cruel? Sure, but it's still cleaner than politics.

2. When your business is slumped and sales have slowed, how important is a proven VP of Sales?

Sure the answer is easy but another question to ask is "how long will you look on your own before bringing in a specialist? Put a pencil to it and determine what it costs to have the wrong sales leader at the top. It's very expensive.

Most top sales talent won't work for the wrong manager, so you get turnover, which costs plenty. If the VP of Sales is taking you in the wrong direction it costs plenty and if they don't have a sense of urgency it really COSTS PLENTY. Most managers hire in their own likeness. So if the VP of Sales is ineffective, there's a good chance the whole team is.

Insiders won't cooperate with ineffective managers, and instead resent them, and stockholders want the head of the CEO. The CEO then decides on the right sales replacement, hopefully not too late.

Although selling is hard work, the right sales leader makes selling look natural and fun. If you've spent a few million in research and development and more on marketing, is it wise not to see who's available from an established recruiter at this time? Headhunters won't demand you hire their candidate, but at least you'll see how your candidate compares! You're welcome to shop a little.

3. When your competition has Michael Jordan selling for them in a critical territory, does it make sense to get him on your team?

Often times, yes! Just make sure the rep can work in your culture. This strategy isn't always recommended unless you're taking from an industry leader.

4. Can you benefit from having independent recruiters always looking for key people for your organization in the market?

I have a great new homebuilder client in the Columbus, Ohio area. Our relationship is such I "keep an eye out" for salespeople I meet who can help his business. Since I'm in the people business he sees benefit in having another pair of eyes in search of resources for his company. Now, he can either hire the salesperson or not, but I've found the better candidates I send him the better the chances he'll make them an offer. He relies on me to send good candidates and I count on him to occasionally bring one in.

5. Does your over-worked HR person have time to source the right sales help for your enterprise?

Can she/he understand what motivates sales people to your product or service? Further, does she/he have time to check references, make a timely offer and have the skill set to sell them on your opportunity? If you think so, then there's a reason your sales are in the toilet, and the reason is YOU! (sorry, but you needed that)

6. *Are you staffed appropriately to take time to run ads, take calls, phone screen, interview two or three times, make the right offer..... to the right candidate.....at the right time so they don't take another offer elsewhere, right when you think you "have them"?*

7. What does it cost you to take time out of your day to hire?

8. What is your business?

If it's technology, then you must be competitive around new technology, manage a bevy of consultants, stay focused on big, hard-to-please clients and then get really good at HIRING THE RIGHT SALES PEOPLE! Sounds difficult and it is. Do what you're good at and hire professionals to do the rest. Technical people understand this because they seem to have invented the thought.

WE LOVE TECHNICAL SEARCHES! Technology creators have bright, potentially huge business plans with large payoffs if they hit. It's satisfying to work with them in their ventures.

9. *What is the true cost of an empty territory?*

Do the math and decide how long you can go without representation in an open territory or even one that is underutilized. If the territory produces one million a year, does it make sense to spend 10k to fill it? A recent client asked for a discount if I found someone really fast for them. I said, shouldn't it be the other way around? If I help stop the bleeding early, shouldn't I get a bonus?

10. Qualified Directors and Vice Presidents who work at American companies don't typically read or certainly respond to the want ads.

There are rejection and confidentiality factors to consider. We've found they aren't necessarily closed to new ideas and if contacted will consider a carefully presented new challenge and opportunity.

11. *Family considerations*

Sometimes it is necessary to meet with family members to ease their fear of change. If a man changes jobs, the entire family, including his wife, parents, and in-laws often must bless the decision. Families are closer now and separating them geographically has never been more challenging.

12. *Recruiters can help build image, brand and customer base*

With many recruiters, candidate lists become potential client lists and vice versa. Our consultants do the job of sales people building your brand and image in the marketplace. We talk with 30 to 50 people on an average search. Communicating to potential managers and sales people in your industry gets mileage for perception of a positive workplace. All of the top 10 firms appearing on Fortune magazines "most admired firms" list also have great brands. The right recruiting firm often builds credibility while assisting in selling your brand image.

Also, recruiters are spreading the word daily to industry insiders who discuss hot companies and opportunities.

13. *It's a well-known fact, people tend to hire in their own likeness. Managers hire people like them. What is your background?*

If it's technical, you're likely to hire a sales person with good technical skills. People with extensive technical skills normally are not the most productive sales people.

Discussing job requirements

This is a key discussion between you and recruiter. How can they get that right person for you when you don't give them all the gory details, nuances, everything important down to personality type. If a recruiter does not take time in this activity, I'd question his ability. He must have the details or cannot be expected to do a proper search.

When recruiters try to communicate what their client is looking for and they didn't get the details, it's purely speculation because they didn't ask key questions. WHY? Because they acted to their client like they knew what to look for. And they will waste time (money) finding near misses without those details. Many recruiters don't want to take the decision makers time with questions they think show incompetence or lack of knowledge. If the hiring manager won't give you time to get all the specs, they might not take time to review your candidate when you get them to the table. The result is time wasted.

The client may say "I need a Director of Sales." So, the recruiter says, "Well I sure know what that is so I don't need to ask stupid questions and tie up the HR gal's time on the phone. That way, she will like me better."

Well, it's better to spend time early on and not have to send unqualified or near miss candidates. And the time wasted over wondering is substantial. It seems like getting back to the hiring manager with those kinds of issues is also uneasy. They wonder, "Why didn't you ask that question earlier?"

Ensure the headhunter is sold on your product or service and can sell it to others...

Can they sell your service to candidates? Recruiters have a 95% closing ratio on offers, and companies without recruiters are at 70%. Clients must be sold on our ability to find quality candidates to work for their organization. And when a candidate is uncertain about the client company you represent you better start selling or you're in trouble.

Yes, recruiting has been called a very advanced sales career because of all the people to appease.

THE CANDIDATE   The job seeker usually wants to move because the new company offers more opportunity than their last position. The candidate must be happy with the offer, the position, location, compensation package, company ethics, support, and potential upward mobility.

THE CANDIDATE'S FAMILY Certainly the spouse must be happy with the geography including the weather, schools, healthcare services, security and churches in the area. He/she must have adequate relocation information, which is usually furnished by the recruiter.

THE CLIENT   (The one who pays us) The business owner wants to know they're getting someone who doesn't do drugs, cheat on their expense reports, drink too much, and say the wrong things to clients. They are hoping to attract candidates who work at least 50 yours per week and make quota. AND attain goal with a good attitude and be easy to manage.

THE CLIENT COMPANY MANAGEMENT TEAM   Here's a special one. It is not only important the hiring manger or owner of a company likes the candidate, but key people in the enterprise they'll interact with.
"The bottom line" is still the bottom line. Without an emissary from your company who has the time, skill set and resources to facilitate a complete search and the knowledge base of "how to" it is difficult to identify, interview effectively, cover all details of reference checking to timely finish the hiring process before sales territories are exhausted or into your competitors hands.

Types of searches

RETAINED Everyone has heard about this type. You get to write a check before you even see a candidate. Recruiters receive a third of the total fee to start researching for the open position. You're then invoiced another third when you interview a pre-set amount of qualified candidates, often two or three. The final payment is due when the candidate starts employment with the company. References are furnished, and most firms include recommendations. The McCandlish Group offers retained searches for less than the 30% that Korn Ferry charges.

CONTINGENCY This is how most searches are completed. The client reviews the search firm's candidates and if the client hires them the average fee of 25% of the employee's first year salary is invoiced. Many recruiters are willing to work in this manner. The downside (for the recruiter) is doing a month's worth of work and the client not interviewing a hot candidate timely so they take a position with another company. It is frustrating because the client may not respond to interview fast enough, make a hiring decision fast enough, or make the right decision for the best candidate. Mistakes are commonly made in this area.

So, let's say the company hires a sales manager they have found, as opposed to hiring the recruiting firm's candidate to save $12,000. The manager has a 3 million goal and hits 2 million. Now, the recruiting firm had a candidate who always hit goal, and that's why they submitted him. Although the client saved $12,000 on the recruiting firm........they lost the potential $800,000 sales volume they felt strongly their candidate should've brought in.

Now, I know this is not a great example if you're on a limited budget for hiring, but know where to save and where to spend. The VP of Sales, for instance, or Director of Sales will be a critical hire if you're building a team. Utilize a search expert for this critical slot and let the new Director of Sales recruit his team. The Director will want some say in future hires since their sales number is usually a team goal.

Is there any real way to know a producer? No, but history is a good indicator. But there's a reason you don't you pull your own teeth, why you don't paint your own car, and why you don't fix your own plumbing. It's certainly because the professionals do it better, faster, and it ends up saving money in the long run.

Another option

Contingency with 14-DAY exclusive is a good way for us to satisfy many clients.   Why? For many reasons, this search benefits both client and The McCandlish Group. The EXCLUSIVE doesn't interfere with our client's efforts. So, if you wish to interview your own people, get referrals from vendors and employees, you can and it doesn't conflict with our agreement.

This type of search only prohibits us from competing with other search firms and possibly spinning our wheels. We have always produced a viable candidate timely on this plan.

This method sets realistic completion schedules and gives us reasonable time for research and identifying the candidate. We'll also endure multiple interviews, check references, review cultural match and schedule interviews with the client. If we haven't performed within the set time frame, you can invite every recruiter in the yellow pages. This search is good for us because we can give retained type service at contingency fees when we have high probability of fulfilling client expectations.

By the way, if you said, I can't gamble, let's fill this territory now, we can oblige. To gain anyone's full attention and get the maximum amount of candidates available a retained search is recommended. That is your guarantee a firm like ours can set aside time on your needs to accommodate you. If you think about it, no one can guarantee results without being paid to work for you. Otherwise the recruiter must start their day asking the question, where can I best make a match today. Who will see my candidates the fastest and follow my advice, or make an offer? It's the real world.

We normally identify a candidate within 5 working days. Our extensive database of proven sales professionals ensures our success. We normally send a qualified sales resume from our firm within 5 business days after a signed search agreement. The rest is contingent on client urgency and available of key personnel involved in the hiring process.

Why a retained search is the best option for high-level sales positions.

When you deal with money matters, do you tell your competitors or make them public? If so, it probably doesn't matter to you what kind of search you perform.

Doesn't the process of sourcing the right VP of Sales really mean money? Of course it does. The process should be discreet and confidential. If your competitors know you are contemplating a replacement, they will take your existing staff because of the uncertainty it represents. Sales people want to know what's going to happen because they don't want to continue prospecting if their efforts will be for naught. Who can guess what a new VP will do? Bring in his/her own people? Eliminate their job? Make them work harder for less by changing the compensation plan?

Salespeople ask those questions when there is questionable leadership. If there is no leadership for a period of time, what then? You could lose your entire staff. And do you want to make it public you're in the hunt for new leadership? Not hardly.

Another thought is whether to promote from within. I'd even consider a consultant's opinion on who is best internally qualified. This represents a whole category I won't address in this publication. Move cautiously when making these changes.

The McCandlish Group will walk you through the entire process of retained search to promptly, professionally source, interview, and position your new sales leader.

INDEPENDENT REPS OR SALES EMPLOYEES

How does formerly being independent affect a rep's motivation to work for my company?

The new marketplace is a setting for entrepreneurs. Sales reps can negotiate and perform as if independent but also be a team player, stay loyal, and build synergy with a team of people. Each individual is different but I've seldom seen independent sales reps that won't consider working on a sales team with great cultural fit in order to obtain a bigger piece of pie. That said, it depends on the WIIFM. The WIIFM is What's In It For Me? If the sales person can get an "unlimited opportunity" as part of a team he'll normally come into the fold. He possibly went out on his own because of an employer that didn't effectively manage sales people. Do you know anyone that doesn't want benefits these days?

Now of course there are other factors of age, need, etc, but in general terms it's ok to hire someone who has been independent, especially in sales. Sales people operate independently anyway but usually enjoy being around others and part of a team.

Employment Trivia

An interesting figure to remember is this. In the 1950's the average stay at a job in the US was 22 years. In 1999 it was 3.6 years.

Six figure earners.... With almost 300 million people in the US, and total employment over 136 million consider almost 7 million hold two jobs. According to Labor Department figures,

US residents that enjoy salaries, commissions and bonuses at the $100,000 level are listed below.

3,512,000 at $100,000-199k	(2.60%)
816,000 at $200-499k	(0.61%)
152,000 at $500-999k	(0.11%)
78,000 at $1M+	(0.06%)

More than 1 million six-figure jobs become available each year. Many take advantage of perks and expenses rather than wages, so I think the number is probably skewed somewhat but this gives a general idea.

Annual turnover in large corporations is approximately 25% and accounts for the vast percentage of six-figure opportunities.

ACCEPTING CANDIDATES FROM OTHER INDUSTRIES
WHEN DOES IT WORK?

1. When you've verified the candidate has a working knowledge of your product line.

How? It could be exposure to the business because it was their spouse's occupation, or their father's

NOT because he/she was in the business way back when and wants to go back. Normally if one leaves an industry once, it's because they didn't like it or weren't well received. Sometimes, though, a change in venue and work associates can revive one's original interest in an industry.

2. When the selling cycle, buyers and dollar amounts are similar.

3. When it's their hobby and they love the product or service. And of course they can communicate reasons why you should let them gamble with your dollars.

Can furniture sales people sell landscaping? Can copier reps sell technology? Are retail sales skills transferable into consulting sales?

No problem. The ability to change jobs was never more obvious than from my career. I changed from selling signs to security systems to office copiers to cellular phones to video distribution to management consulting services to outplacement services to recruiting.

If someone has performed as a sales achiever in a different industry and they earnestly want to sell the product you offer for personal reasons, THEY PROBABLY CAN.

If they are being called passionately, they may be a great hire.

If you need to analyze their ability, try this.

Was their background B to B? Some sales people do better with the consumer than to other businesses. Also, consider that many sales people gravitate to B-B because they learned how to sell in a B-C environment and left because of the hours. Get a commitment here that hours won't be the issue. You'll probably have to guess for them if they can handle it. Is the guy with three kids who play soccer going to be around on the weekend? Doubt it.

Did they sell 8 or 10 of a product monthly or did they sell a product that's purchased every three months? Some reps need constant "hits" of success or they lose interest. A long cycle makes them impatient and they lose focus.

Was their product technical with a long learning curve? If so, they may be the patient type who needs a longer selling cycle. They may sell 4 deals a year and do $1,000,000. If you're asking this person to switch gears and sell weekly then consider that might not be their style. They won't close often enough which is necessary in a shorter cycle.

A recent mistake on my part was to place a vacuum cleaner salesman into a new home sales opportunity. The situation created the only time in my career I had to replace a candidate who didn't fulfill the guarantee period of 60 days. I thought if a guy could sell vacuum cleaners for 13 years, he could sell anything. As it happened, he didn't like the process of seeing a potential buyer 6 times before they bought from him. He was so used to a first time close, he was impatient for the longer process necessary to sell a home.

Some sales people are strong at creating an emotional buy. That is a very short selling cycle, sometimes as in office equipment or in home sales, and possibly car sales.

CANDIDATES FROM OUTPLACEMENT FIRMS?????

If a job candidate has engaged a firm that advised them on resume issues, interviewing skills, and how to market themselves, don't discount them because they have sought assistance in their job search. On the contrary, I'd give them extra points for effort. Obtaining advice shows commitment to career and making themselves more marketable in a competitive environment.

There are many who think sales candidates should be able to find a job on their own. Sure, most can and do.

If, through an outside agency, a sales person can find cool, fun gigs to make them want to work endless hours, feel passion over products or services of a fast growing company, then that is all positive. The agency has assisted a portion of the market that contacts recruiters daily for help. Although those services don't "make a match", they improve the candidate's chances substantially.

Don't we all need an outside opinion on our business and even personal lives once in a while? Besides, the marketing effort alone can uncover opportunities an individual can seldom find.

I mention it here because it's an affordable option for businesses to provide job search assistance for employees who have contributed in the past but are no longer part of the company plan.

WHY SALES CONSULTING AS PART OF RECRUITING?

Often, hiring managers will say, "just find me an aggressive sales type. I can't find anyone that can close or that really wants to work."

Translated, this normally means, "We don't do a great job of managing salespeople, don't understand them and just want them to do what they're hired to do; sell something."

Although big companies seem to have a better handle now on how to motivate salespeople, there still is an underlying attitude among non-sales types that sales people make too much and do too little. They work in an unstructured environment and name their own hours. Then you always hear when someone makes a huge sale, as everyone is envious. Many companies cut salespeople's territories, commissions and potential because of the jealousies that are created, not because it improves the business.

Now, back to the original question, *"Why consulting as part of recruiting?"*

Consider these thoughts.

Recruiters want to make sure they aren't putting candidates into impossible situations for them to survive. We want to make sure the company has a viable sales process that promotes fair opportunities and is profitable for the company.

I'm proposing you share your sales process with your recruiter and get an outsider's viewpoint of it. Sales recruiters can advise on process and if something is out of line, advise you. You can then decide to make a change or not. This also gives recruiters tremendous insight when sourcing the right sales candidates for your team.

Are you hiring for a new territory? Does the company have a customer base in the territory or is there missionary work involved to open new doors? If so, that's fine. Just give an honest assessment of the situation so the new sales representative knows what to expect. This will reduce turnover.

Recently a client software developer said they wanted to grow to new markets. They mentioned the next stop was New York City because a marketing professional said the pickings were ripe for their product.

The IS Manager said, "What do you think?"

Isn't if funny how the good ones always say that? Rather than "we're going to do this, this and that?" And months later, after blowing their budget, wondering what they were thinking.

I said, "New York is tough. It's expensive to do business there and many companies have their best representation there. Selling is one thing but support people have to get around the city, pay for transportation, and deal with highly competitive situations. Since competitors have their top sales pros and support systems there, why not consider another approach?"

If you target easier geography to acquire market share than the Big Apple, when you finally go there you'll have cash flow for the bumps in the road. Because of the size of the market alone, generating cash flow can take longer than expected. If that's the case why place the company in jeopardy over success or failure there?

The middle markets like Austin, Columbus, Charlotte, and Baltimore, are much safer and when you get positive cash flow, the right marketing plan, and many new client referrals, take on THE CITY! Once we've reviewed your budget and marketing plan I'll be able to better advise but I wouldn't go there for the first office."

Now who knows what they will do, we've just given them food for thought. If their company had a steady revenue stream and was ready for New York, the advice would have been different.

Often, expansion can follow existing sales talent. If you have a "hitter" who has an established base in a marketplace, and it's a viable market, why not start there? He's a known commodity. Build around his network.

THIS IS OUR VALUE-ADD FOR CLIENTS

Free sales consulting! This service seems to separate our firm from other recruiters. I've shopped the web and just haven't found companies offering this service. Technology based organizations often contact us for compensation and incentive ideas.

Not all our clients take advantage of this offer. Many are established and just want us to quickly find sales producers. They do realize this knowledge base gives us advantages in sourcing their next VP of Sales or CEO as well as filling sales territories with account executives.

It's perfect timing when someone says I've turned over some key people, what should I do? The right thing is to get an outside perspective from experts on that issue. We can pick up one or two process flaws to improve and move on.

Those conversations are free anyway. Consulting ideas are not invoiced with our firm because we need to develop a successful atmosphere for sales people we place. Turnover is not good for most organizations but when it happens let's look at the problem, brainstorm solutions and get back to the business of selling.

New stars can be found and sometimes less expensively than bidding for them from your competitors. But, let's capture that moment of despair to evaluate the system.

Let's get an understanding of why you're turning over people. Is it the management style of an existing manager? Is it a competitor who is taking them? Don't you want to know?

Recently, in the middle of a Director of Sales search for a builder, I find that another company has a process that is interesting. They have added one person in their process and it has added 25% to their gross sales numbers. Almost as important, sales people within the system are thrilled to have this additional support person and the whole enterprise is moving forward exponentially.

If your competitors were doing something similar wouldn't it be nice to know?

This service is offered by our firm at no charge. Why? Because when it's over, my clients are in a place to grow sales and when they grow sales, guess who makes more placements? ......my kids DADDEE?

If your sales and marketing isn't getting you what you want, does it make sense to get an outsider's opinion?

Experienced recruiters normally know how businesses operate. In our situation, we have advised hundreds on sales process. When they say WE CAN'T KEEP SALESPEOPLE, I ask many questions about process to help them evaluate their sales results, to better compete and sometimes just to stay in business.

These questions don't always result in hiring more sales people. More often the result is changing methodology or hiring the right sales candidate.

Why, you ask, since I'd be better off financially if I just keep replacing sales people for them?   Not so. If the client can't keep salespeople they won't be around to hire us at all. They need help to grow and with the right process in place the company will be profitable. That's the only way it works.

MAKING AN OFFER

By the way, salary discussion and salary negotiation are two different issues. Discussion should happen early to determine if the company could afford the candidate. Negotiation usually happens before a written offer is made. That way time isn't spent on rewriting offers.

When it's time to make an offer, resist the temptation to do so without thinking it through. In a competitive environment for a top candidate it's easy to get caught up in the moment and shoot from the hip. Write down specifics of position responsibilities, territory (if appropriate), sales goals, and minimum level of productivity and results.

Even top sales pros are not known for properly researching sales opportunities thoroughly. Career and industry direction are not always in the forefront. Many are "hunters" and they've found another opportunity. They'll sell you on them and then decide if they want the position or not.

Invariably when they say, "C'mon Mr. Sales Manager, when can I start?" And the sales manager says, "right away. How about Monday?" The sales candidate could say, "It sounds great and I'm excited about it, but let me talk with my wife. I'm sure you understand, I'll call you in a few days."

Stay in CONTROL. Now, who's in control of that situation? The candidate. And they just sold you like any other prospect.

A better scenario might be..... when they ask for the job, say, "If we were to extend an offer how much time would you need? or....."Are you contemplating other offers right now?"

If no, then possibly, "I need to think about this for a day or so. Then I will contact you to discuss an offer. You are someone we are interested in, and as soon as I consult with some others I'll call you. I sincerely appreciate your interest and we'll talk soon."

CAUTION. Make the offer when it's good timing for you but remember; if you want the candidate, tell them, and let them know you're just working out the details. Otherwise they have no reason to stick around and wait. Many high caliber candidates will see hesitation here as being unsure.

When I'm getting sold by the best candidates in the business, I just smile because it reassures me they'll sell when hired by companies who hire me. If they don't sell me, I pass, never to return. I can't take a chance they'll not perform and I'll have to replace them with another candidate. That's time wasted for my client and me.

Important aspects candidates consider seem to be the following:
1. Do I like these people and can we work together?
2. Do I trust them?
3. Is the opportunity unlimited, as the company suggests?

Once a decision to hire is reached by the hiring manager, our lead consultant communicates the verbal job offer to the finalist candidate so that any negotiating can be handled by the search firm and take place at arms length between the client and candidate. Once the verbal job offer is accepted, the client prepares a written offer. Without a written offer, a verbal offer may later be rejected if all wasn't explained and understood. You cannot verify the specifics of an offer that is not written.

The offer should include the following:

Start Date
Friendly, welcome communication, personalized

Expectations

Exact compensation including bonuses; is bonus calculated on net or gross? How bonus accrues, equity or stock options

Relocation, include moving allowance

Health Insurance, vacation time, educational benefits

The search assignment is now complete and the real work for the new employee and hiring manager begins!

Generally, a retained search should take about 45-60 days to be completed. Often the process can move much faster. We have found that the process moves the fastest when the hiring manager and team are closely aligned on their expectations about what they want to see in the hired candidate---so a good position spec that everyone supports and endorses at the outset is crucially important.

We normally identify the candidate within a week to ten days. It seems to take 30 days in the interviewing process, including gaining each decision maker's buy-in of the candidate, which takes the rest of the time mentioned.

Your written job offer eliminates misunderstandings and clarifies important details. Use this opportunity to make the applicant feel positive about employment with you. In discussing the offer, be careful not to imply more than you can deliver. Also, you may want to use this letter to ask for proof of legal employment eligibility in case of restrictive employment agreements.

What happens if the candidate rejects an offer?

In five years, The McCandlish Group has seldom had a candidate refuse an offer. Recruiters manage expectations along the way. Early on, we get "what if" commitments. We ask, "If the client offers this, are you ok with that?" A salary range is established with the candidate that is already cleared by the client. Since our communication involves getting commitments from the candidate in these "what if" scenarios, we know in advance "if" and "what" the candidate will accept before we advise clients to make an offer. Recruiters will also know the candidates other activity to gauge how fast their clients should move.

Companies that have a rejection-of-offer problem need to self-analyze and find solutions internally. I've noticed that managers and internal recruiters are too tolerant when a candidate rejects an offer. It's typical for managers to blame the recruiter, the candidate, or be acceptance of the fact that "those things happen."

Rather than accept what they consider inevitable, instead study each rejection scientifically to identify the real reasons why offers are rejected. Acceptance rates naturally go up as the economy goes down, but it's important for managers and recruiters to remain vigilant for average applicants, because the cost of a rejection in a key position can easily exceed $10,000. Great recruiters have offer acceptance rates of over 95%, and that's no accident when the average rate is often below 70%.

The offer as science

Many managers and recruiters look at the recruiting process as an art. That approach guarantees a low success rate -- because putting together and making a great offer is really a science. By doing your research and collecting data, you can dramatically improve the content of each offer you make.

It takes more than improving the actual offer letter itself to get the highest acceptance rates. Look at the whole interview and selection process as a customer relationship management (CRM) problem. Once you realize that this is really a sales issue, and that successfully making an offer and selling a customer are similar processes, you'll see that you are merely trying to sell a customer (candidate), and trying to close the deal with a yes.

Just like in sales, it requires a combined customer service and sales approach. Every other approach is just guesswork.

Take steps to find out why your offers are rejected

There are a variety of approaches to investigating why offers are rejected. Remember, top performers look for something significantly different than what average performers look for, so be sure to segment your data collection between the two. "Reason finding" tools and techniques include:

Ask new hires what worked

On their first day of the job, ask new hires which specific elements of their offer
a) were the most compelling,
b) had no impact, and
c) almost caused them to reject the offer.
Use this data to redesign the content of your offers to better fit their needs and expectations.

Review competitive offers

Also ask new hires on their first day for reasons why they rejected other company offers and bought in to yours. Compare others' offers to see where your packages are strong or weak.

Post-reject surveys

Most candidates tell you "it was the money." It's a great excuse, because it generally absolves managers and internal recruiters of all blame. Unfortunately, it's generally not factually true...it's just an effective excuse. If you really want to find out why candidates reject your offers, ask them three or six months later why they turned you down. There are several market research firms that will do this for you, and the results, almost universally, show that it was not "the money." If a recruiter is involved, they should know the real reason, so ask to prevent losing future prospects.

Utilize the research of others

Identifying what excites employees in a job is not difficult. The Gallup organization has done extensive research on the subject.

Almost all of the satisfaction factors are controlled exclusively by the line manager. Seventy-five to eighty-five percent of the reasons that make offers and jobs compelling are controlled directly by the supervising manager. Common satisfaction factors include two-way communication, growth and learning, flexibility and control on what they work on, whom they work with, and when and where the work is done.

SALES DIRECTORS AS CONSULTANTS/ CONTRACTORS

The McCandlish Group is adept at sourcing short-term sales advisors on contract. A practice increasing in popularity is Temp-to-Perm hiring agreements. The candidate is hired as a contractor and the potential employer gets to "try before they buy" the candidate. This is a practice popular in the IT field and healthcare but has also enjoyed success in other areas.

For some business owners it's considered a negative to release competitive information to consultants or people outside their business. To address that issue our consultants sign a non-disclosure before taking an assignment. Clients also interview our consultants and do their own reference checks occasionally.

The only negative for the candidate is the stigma of them accepting consulting work instead of being an employee. When someone reviews his or her resume the contractor has to explain a non-employee activity.

That said, it is often a good situation for the employer to have a sales and marketing pro come in. *It is actually less expensive than hiring an outside consulting firm to implement changes.* Our sales advisor is on staff working as Director of Sales on your behalf instead of just advising you. It's a viable option for start up organizations that want to test the waters before they commit to hiring a high level sales leader with no familiarity.

As interim manager, if you like the way the consultant manages, you may hire them. Many candidates won't enter into this type of relationship because they feel they won't have been granted full authority as a temporary hire. It usually works best if management backs the move publicly to their team.

Companies can save mind-share on exit strategies, stock option plans, automobile leases, country club memberships, tuition re-imbursement, and enjoy trying before they buy, so to speak, until they can make an offer.........after the consultant has proven themselves. IF the consultant gets them through a tight phase, they may then hire the consultant as a full time employee.

When it's appropriate

Granted, most of the time, a free consultation from our group and subsequent search for permanent placement is the norm. But, if you are in transition, want someone to implement sales presentations, establish procedural guidelines in an employee handbook, manage existing teams without losing momentum, or have urgent management needs, hiring an independent consultant is a viable option.

SUCCESSFUL SEARCHES, STORIES, SOLUTIONS

A recent search for a VP of Sales for a cellular billing software company is a good example of how our service works. A technology expert, IS Manager contacted me through a referral. The company he represented was a start-up with some cash flow, around one million a year. With only ten employees, they asked me to review their infrastructure and advise on their plan to add sales staff and grow. They had just made a high-dollar sale and wanted to finance their growth through the cash flow it provided.

He did not mention at that time a search was impending or our services may be necessary at a later date, but needed some guidance on where, when and how to add sales staff. My referral source said I would help and not charge them.

The analysis included planning how many sales people they needed to add and in what amount of time to do 7 million in annual sales for 2004. Part of the process was to set goals based on how many product trials the company should potentially do in a quarter. We then determined closing ratios on the trials to assign sales goals. We took the average sale per trial and decided the rep should sell 3-4 systems the first year at an average of $400,000 each and 4-6 the second. Based on that potential we also derived that competitively we'd have to pay a salary of around $80,000 for an account executive that could add another $80,000 in commissions if he sold 2 million in products and services at a commission rate of 4%.

Other considerations were where to open the first office and what level of sales experience should staff it.

A couple weeks later they called and said, we're ready to hire some people, have any ideas? I said "sure".

The IS Manager and founder/CEO gave me some requirements and I went to work. I contacted industry associates, set up Internet postings, listed the opening on a recruiter's network and began recruiting from other software companies. The network of 1400 recruiters assists each other in furnishing candidates and act as search partners for openings.

After many discussions and three interviews, they offered my candidate a position as VP of Sales. He will add one sales executive to his region in Chicago, duplicate the effort in Columbus, Ohio and once cash flow is established, they'll open another market.

Another software firm was just getting established and had developed a great technical solution in the Internet Security segment of IT.

They had issues with a sales manager who wasn't making quota and wondered how to treat it. The employee was to be the Director of Sales and was coincidentally the founder's brother. What does one do with his brother when he doesn't make quota? Worse yet, the brother had a contract that (he thought) made him an equity partner.

The founder was wise to include some results parameters around his brother's participation and since he didn't get the sales numbers they agreed on, the agreement was null and void.

Legal opinions aren't our expertise, but I do have experience in sales agent and employee agreements. After advising them I mentioned they might also want to contact an attorney who specializes in contract law.

They weren't invoiced for the opinion but I gave them an overview of how I would treat the sales manager and options to consider. The option included moving the sales manager to a channel management responsibility that seemed a better match for his personality and they would still benefit from his client relationships, and probably save litigation at this critical time.

The sales manager wasn't adept at opening new accounts and generally wasn't producing new clients. He did have some existing relationships that were critical for the short term since VC's were evaluating them as a viable investment. Not a good time to rock the boat with personnel issues.

The sales manager was better at developing strategic relationships. Often sales performers are misplaced for position. At last word, he was performing much better in this capacity. It was a win-win as both company and employee are productive and moving on. The wrong decision may have lead to litigation instead of this less volatile approach.

Knowing how salespeople will react to executive decisions is part of the drill here. We guessed correctly the sales manager would take a lateral role and stay with the group.

When it came time to search for a new VP of Sales to drive the direct field force, the manager called and said, "We'd like you to find someone to direct sales functions and lead us. They need to open new accounts, establish new markets, manage others, handle clients, solve problems of smooth delivery and implementation and grow. AND we need them now.

After 30 days, the right candidate was identified and they came to an agreement soon after. I'm now working with them to evaluate which new markets to attack first with key software sales pros nationally that require little management and understand urgency.

The company is growing quickly and I feel plugged in since I was there from the beginning. Now I know what, when and who they need, since matching individual personality types is important.

We've also structured a contract fee agreement that fits their cash flow needs since paying full price for recruiting is difficult in a high growth operation.

It's not discounting, just adjusting for exclusive, volume business. The company has given me an exclusive and I earn it. When they say, find someone for Chicago, I work non-stop until I have the right candidate. Then, they do their part by making the interview a priority and saying yes or no. Either is fine, but any decision is better than no decision. If they are uncertain about a candidate, I supply another. Uncertainty means no to me.

There are two words printed boldly on the board in my office that I live by.

THOSE WORDS ARE ....NAIL IT!

Find Michael Jordan! When you find the right candidate, life is easier for both you and client. The conversation goes from "Do we bring this person in now?" or "Can we afford this person now?" to "Wonder if this guy will take our offer?" Different mindset, huh?

The best advice I ever received from any headhunter was to nail it, find the best candidate in the market today. AND, as in any sales cycle, doing the work up front makes it easier in the end.

We work with a top ranked pharmaceutical company who has sincere challenges getting back to us with any information about candidate submittals.

It's hard to understand when that happens. Granted, we're not privileged to know what HR professionals go through with hiring managers as miscommunication or no communication often happens. But when we're working on the contingency that we find a qualified candidate, which means no pay unless we find someone that their HR people can't find, then we'd like some acknowledgement. Was he the right match? Did he have the skill set you need? Can you work with the candidate? Was there a cultural match? AND what did I miss so I hit it the next time.

My associates would be more motivated if we were encouraged and informed. I know the pharma HR people resent having to pay us fees when they feel qualified to search. They usually don't have time for searching for one top candidate. And they have to constantly fight budget issues. We know their supervisors ask, "Do we pay the headhunters for this candidate or hire the one we found?" It's often an issue.

On a contingency search, we know big companies will hire our candidate as a last resort. We HAVE to send a close match for their requirements and the best candidate.

At least get back to us with feedback. It's courtesy! Besides, we may be free until we source the right candidate for you, but your level of service will improve when communication improves.

Our percentages are high. Approximately 50% of the candidates interviewed from us receive an offer. We try to do most of the research before a candidate is submitted. References are contacted before we submit someone these days. That's something I didn't do in my early days. We felt just "finding" the right candidate was difficult enough. It is, but normally sending the reference with the submittal pays dividends.

Communication is the key to our business and yours if you're utilizing recruiters. When I executed searches for IBM openings, most of their internal recruiters, although intelligent and competent, were not willing to stick their neck out for a candidate submitted by recruiters. Their continued response was, "The hiring manger hasn't let me know yet."

I kept moving around via referrals from internal recruiters until I found one who sounded like a sales person. She spoke in short sentences and said "I'll call the hiring manager now. If he doesn't get back to me, I'll call the managing principle. We need these slots filled." WHOA, I thought. Here we go.

In a two-month period I placed three security consultants with IBM and at last glance, they were still there, four years later. By the way, sales backgrounds are great for internal recruiters also because they are results oriented, get their questions answered and gain closure on conversations, deadlines, and expectations.

A $70 million manufacturer in the Columbus area is known for quality, innovation and design capabilities. We replaced a regional sales manager for them on the West Coast. The RSM managed rep firms for the company and didn't hit goal by a long shot. He was overdue to be introduced to his next opportunity.

After our analysis, the founder decided it better to restructure the sales function here with a Director of Sales rather than another RSM and streamline the operation. He was thinking all along it was the right thing to do and when we corroborated it, he made the move.

Many manufacturers I've worked with treat their employees very well. Often they treat salespeople the same as the rest of the team. Now, please don't misinterpret what I'm saying. I'm not saying salespeople are more valuable than engineers, administrators, receptionists, technicians or anyone in the enterprise. BUT, since they are compensated very differently, they should be treated differently. Don't they work independently, away from the office? That's different than most. Do they punch a time clock? That's different than others. Do they have to start when everyone else does? NO! Do they quit when everyone else does? Of course not, so why does everyone try to treat salespeople like everyone else in their enterprise? THEY WORK DIFFERENTLY SO YOU HAVE TO MANAGE THEM DIFFERENTLY!

I cringe when business owners say "We can't offer trips for sales people when we don't offer them for our other employees!"

Could you tell your engineers they need to work 50 hours a week for half their wages and when their finished product gets to market and the money is collected they will get paid the other half? Would your engineers do that? Probably not. But sales people do. Should they be treated the same? I think not. I'm sure there are differing views out there. But, the successful sales operations I've worked for and with manage salespeople differently.

A quick story to share

I'm now working on a search classified as "urgent' by the VP of HR at a 300 million manufacturer who says they have had an open position for one year and need help.

We submitted the perfect candidate according to them and we agreed. They took over two weeks to phone interview the candidate and another week to schedule a face-to-face interview. He has two other companies ready to make an offer. The interviewing HR manager says she is too busy to see this person who could make her life easier if on staff.

This is the most frustrating part of our world. We get a search authorization, find the right candidate and the company cannot move to interview or make an offer.

My message is that our day is filled with RE-PRIORITIZING for clients who don't. We have to ask ourselves each day, who is most likely to see our candidates today?

COMPENSATION

I'm presently establishing relationships with business incubators at universities around the country because of the excitement and energy around new technology ventures. I'll always love an entrepreneurial start-up. From an opportunity standpoint alone, people are motivated and hope abounds. The often-asked question from start-up technology companies is "what should we pay sales talent?" Here are some ideas.

This compensation plan was just finalized in Central Ohio for a fast-growing software developer. Of course technology carries higher salaries than most industries, comparatively.

Position	Base salary	Goal	Commissions	Bonus
Software Sales	$80,000	2 mil	4%-6%	2% over 2 MIL
Director of Sales	$90-$130,000	(team)	2%	.5% above goal
VP Sales	$140-175,000	(team)	2% range	% gross profit

Sales pros that also manage rep firms earn additional commissions from 1% to 5% depending on what other responsibilities are expected. Accelerators can be utilized for quota busters for additional incentive.

VP's and Directors usually receive stock as signing incentive and ability to continue earning on profitable sales numbers. Although it's normally in the form of options, they're distributed at a low price with a vesting period of at least three years.

The practice of using stock options as incentive is one of the most powerful tools ever created for salespeople. They will work for less salary (guarantee) when a share of the pie is available. The old saying is "give them a share and they'll care".

Big companies do less of that now that fewer start-ups exist, and they don't have to. But the new ventures that utilize shares of stock as incentive to create wealth for sales pros, can recruit competitors top talent even though salary and "guarantee" is less.

We invite inquiries for free compensation ideas for sales performers in any industry.

Finally, I'll leave you some thoughts to consider while hiring sales candidates for your organization.

Gold Nuggets

1. Sell more next week than last. You'll never need a long-term plan!

2. Hire for attitude, drive and need. Not for product knowledge. People are sharp and most motivated when facing new opportunities and learning. Are they motivated to sell for you?

3. When interviewing, ask "What was your best sales accomplishment" and if the candidate doesn't smile and get a glow in their eye as they speak, DON'T HIRE THEM!

4. If a sales candidate doesn't tell you why you should hire them, DON'T HIRE THEM!

5. If the candidate is not visibly excited or upbeat about your opportunity, DON'T HIRE THEM.

6. Try to keep your stars, create new challenges for them to grow. It's ok to cut them a better deal than the other reps who sell less. But remember, no one is bigger than the company.

7. Cut or scrutinize the bottom third of your sales staff, regularly. Spend time with the stars and proportionately less on the mid-range producers. Don't try to change the dynamics of why the mid-range can't catch the stars. Some will, some won't, NEXT! Just keep hiring and cut from the bottom.

8. Listen to the candidate who says, "I know I can do this and I really want to". Even if he/she's short on background, desire can overcome inexperience.

9. Growth companies can't normally afford staff to recruit only. HR is a different skill-set than headhunting.

HR often acts as an internal recruiter while handling other duties. Identifying the right candidate is very time consuming and unless they have worked in the discipline of sales, they will be spinning their wheels.

By the way

10. Never hire IBM types (big company) as VP of Sales or CEO unless they have engineered through a startup or two. I like the street-smart sales dog that has had to cold call, scratch, bite and pinch for a deal. If they haven't managed without a huge support function, BE CAREFUL!

11. The McCandlish Group will occasionally accept stock in lieu of cash payment for services. It makes us a partner with vested interests in your success. Each situation is different and I'll be glad to discuss this option.

When you get frustrated by hiring sales people or need free assistance relating to sales process, compensation issues, evaluating internal and external candidates, call The McCandlish Group.

When I founded The McCandlish Group, my goal was to distinguish us in the marketplace by offering complimentary services to enhance our executive search offerings.

There are many professional recruiters who can source sales candidates for you. We differ in that we have actually achieved sales quota in the disciplines we source for. I've actually worked in 7 different industries; hiring, training, and managing over 1000 sales representatives in my career.

Consequently, we can advise you on sales process, compensation, direction and methodologies to build your sales teams, at no charge!

Do you currently have solutions for the following questions?

- We're developing growth strategies for sales teams. Where and when do we open the next office?
- What sales manager skill set is best for this time period of our growth?
- Do we need to name a VP of Sales now or can we find Directors who will "chase the carrot" to be rewarded after they've proven themselves?
- Can you find someone who has "done it before" at a similar company as ours?
- Who can hit the ground running and open doors immediately?
- What are cash needs for driving the sales team?
- Are our sales projections realistic?
- What are realistic goals and incentive plans for sales staffing?

Did it sound like I started selling in this last few pages? I did. I know of no other way. Have you engaged anyone's services who didn't want your business? Me neither.

We'd love to assist you in growing your company! Contact us at 614-766-1800, or visit our website at **www.mccandlishgroup.** com.   Best of luck and good selling!

116